I0494447

Spiritual Light

The Stained Glass of Marc Chagall in Pocantico Hills, New York and Tudeley, Kent

MARTHA RICHARDS

Spiritual Light
Copyright © 2015 Martha Richards

SozoPrint
SozoPrint.com

ISBN 978-0-9929404-1-6

With thanks to …

The helpful staff at Union Church, Pocantico Hills and the Reverend Paul DeHoff.

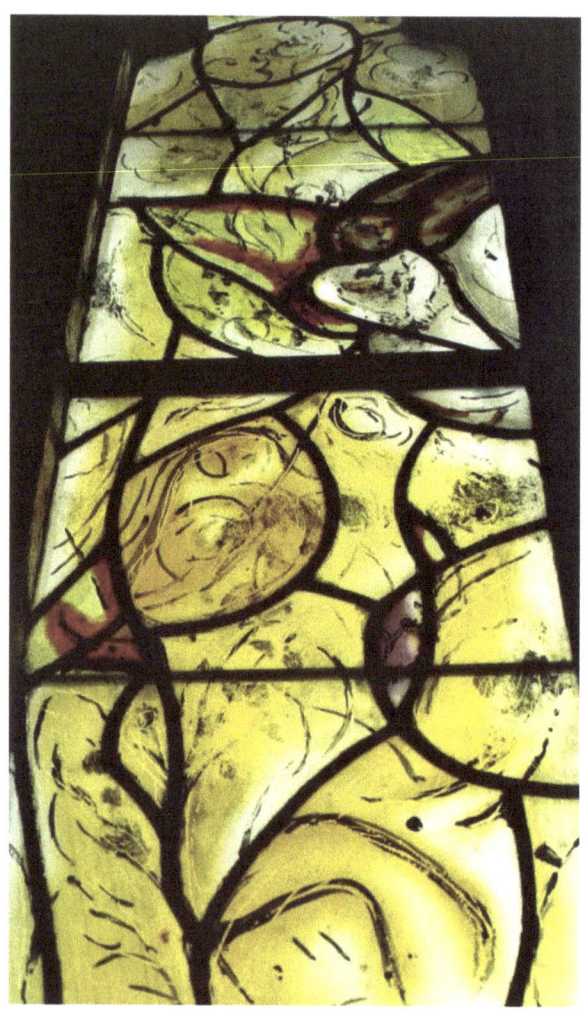

*Detail from one of the yellow abstract windows created
by Chagall and found at All Saints Church, Tudeley*

Contents

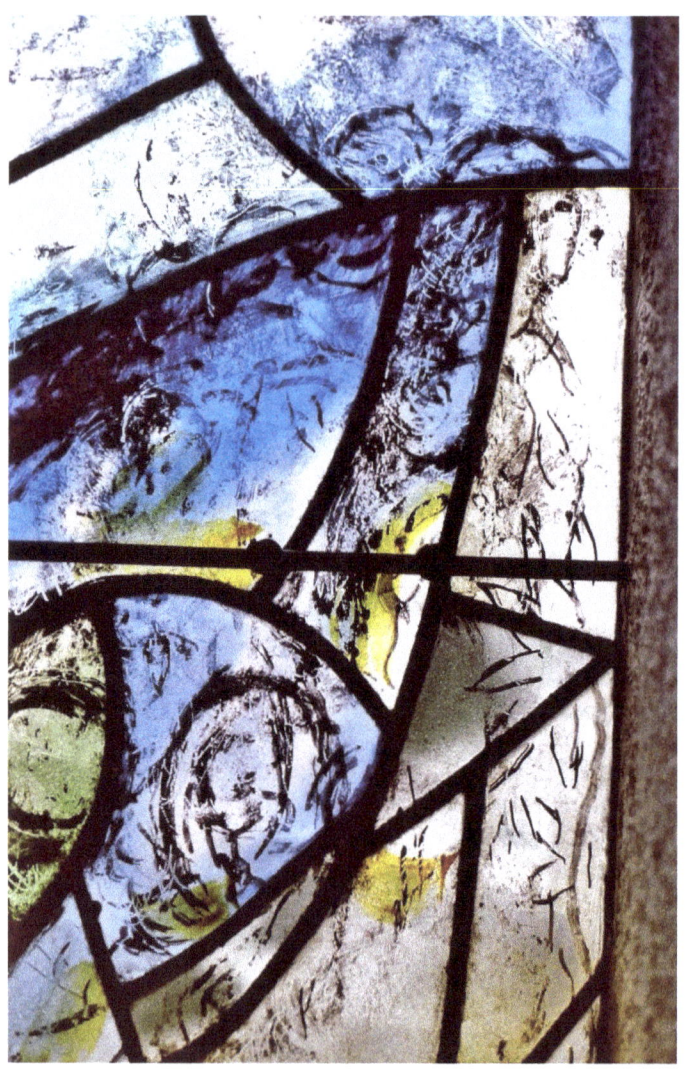

Detail showing a variety of techniques Chagall used in applying the grisaille to his stained glass

Introduction

James Johnson Sweeney has often been quoted: 'If you ask Chagall to explain his paintings, even today he will still reply: "I don't understand them at all. They are not literature. They are merely a pictorial arrangement of images that obsess me ..."[1]

To create a universal understanding of Chagall's paintings, mosaics, tapestries, etchings and stained glass for everyone is not what he would have wished. Chagall would have wanted the individual to find their own meaning, inspiration and understanding when they look at his work. He said:
"Everyone must choose the symbolism for themselves. Judge me by my form and colour."[2]

In this essay I mean to tell you of what his stained glass in All Saints Church, Tudeley, Kent, England and Union Church, Pocantico Hills, New York, America symbolise to me.

Chagall's own religion plays a vital role in finding the symbolism in his windows. He knew of the problems that people have in coming to a place of spiritual enlightenment. He was consistent and inspired in the way he found of aiding them. Chagall's stained glass takes you to a place of revelation by means of movement through a space in both form and colour. The light flowing through the windows takes you on a spiritual journey. They expose your thoughts to other things than just the material and enlightenment is received.

My love of Chagall's stained glass all began quite by accident. In my first year at university, a project was set, dealing with the issue of death. I knew that stained glass dealt a great deal with death and found that Marc Chagall had designed a nearby window commemorating a girl who had died.

I first visited Tudeley with very ordinary, preconceived ideas of what I would find. I was only told that the windows were wonderful pieces of work. When I saw them, I not only had to agree with this description but believed that they had been under estimated on all accounts. Chagall had dealt with the issue of death in a sensitive and honouring way.

Seeing the windows first hand in both church buildings was a valuable experience. These windows have only briefly been written about and reproductions that are available, although a useful as a secondary source are not always pictorially honest. The secondary sources that are available for research were often very basic and did not always express the richness of these pieces. Many people have mentioned Chagall's work at Tudeley in numerous books on stained glass, and even books in books about Chagall, but it seemed that the windows received only a mention.

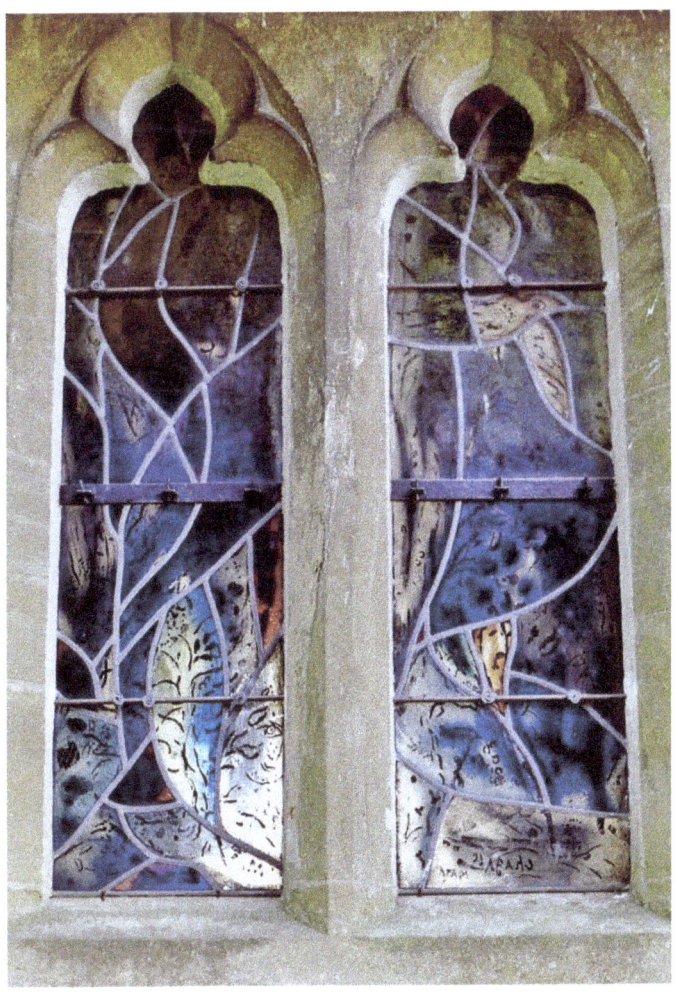

*The possible self-portrait in one of the abstract
windows at Tudeley: bottom left in the left hand panel.*

Stained glass is very difficult to represent in a two dimensional form like a photograph because stained glass affects a three dimensional space. For example, before visiting Pocantico Hills, New York, in the fall, September 1996, I researched a great deal, wrote to the pastor of the church and obtained reproductions of the windows in the form of postcards, magazine and book articles. I went with a certain expectation of what I would find. What I encountered was a fantastic surprise. The items that I had previously gathered did not do Chagall and his windows justice. The windows were far more beautiful. It was an incredible sight to see them all in one place, all having a dramatic affect in one space and each other.

First I will take you to each of the spaces and describe them. Each narrative will be closely followed or include portraits of the stained glass by Chagall.

At Pocantico Hills, the building and grounds will be looked at separate to the windows, whereas Tudeley will be studied as a whole. This becomes an obvious form in which to represent the works because of the diverse ways in which Chagall creates the spiritual journey through the windows in each building.

The conclusion will include comparisons of the building types, environment and most importantly the windows. The question of the significance and relevance of modern stained glass, and in particular, the work of Chagall in these two buildings, shall be answered.

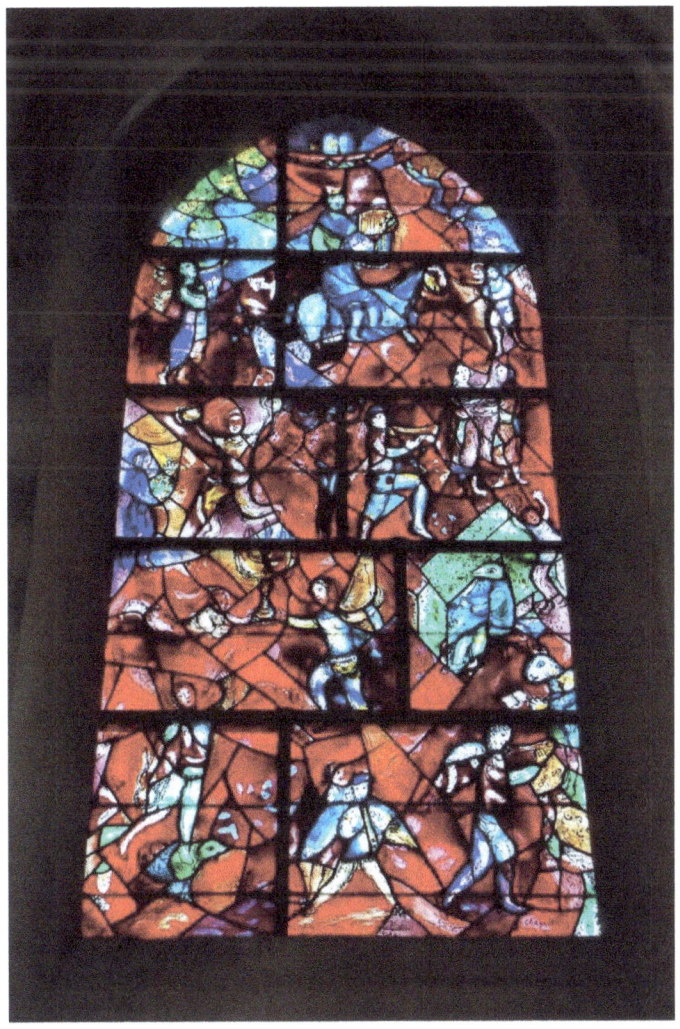

"O praise God in his holiness … let everything that has breath, praise the Lord."
Psalm 150
Chichester Cathedral

Chronological Order* of Chagall's Stained Glass

1958   Chagall meets Charles Marq, master glass maker, they become friends. Created designs for Metz Cathedral.

1960   Designs the Twelve Tribes of Israel for the Synagogue of the Hadassah-Hebrew University, just outside Jerusalem.
Exhibition of Metz Cathedral stained glass held at Reims museum.

1961   Twelve Tribes of Israel exhibited at the Musee des Arts Decoratifs in Paris, and then moved to the Museum of Modern Art in New York from November to January 1962.

1962-63   Metz Cathedral north apse and north transept windows installed.

1964   United Nations memorial window to Dag Hammarsjold in New York entitled Peace. Union Church, Pocantico Hills in Tarrytown, New York state installs The Good Samaritan in memory of John D Rockefeller Jr.

1966   Eight more windows executed for the Pocantico Hills church.

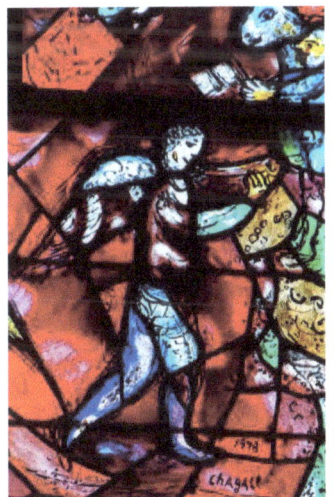
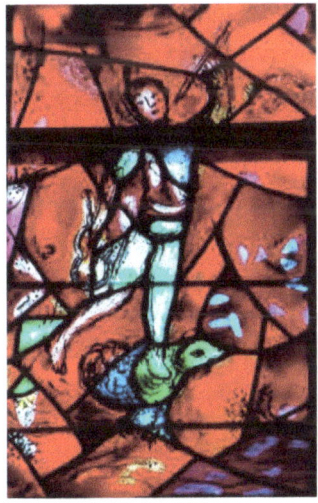

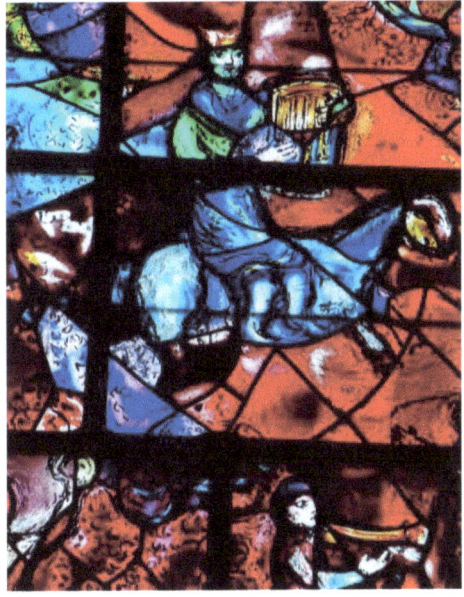

Details from Psalm 150
Chichester Cathedral

13

1967   Memorial to Sarah d'Avigdor Goldsmid in All
        Saints Church, Tudeley in Kent.

1968   Another window for Metz Cathedral.

1969   Seven more windows completed for All Saints
        Church Tudeley, Kent. However, not installed
        until later.

1970   Window for the choir at the Fraumunster in
        Zurich.

1971   Last four windows for All Saints Church,
        Tudeley. Windows still not installed.

1972   The Creation of the World, a series of windows
        for the Musee National Message Biblique in
        Nice.

1974   Windows dedicated in October, All Saints
        Church, Tudeley, Kent.
        Fifteen windows for the central choir at Reims
        Cathedral are unveiled.
1975   Designs a window for the Chapel of Penitents
        in Sarrebourg.

1978   Saint-Etienne in Mayence unveils a window by
        Chagall.
        Psalm 150 is portrayed in the window unveiled
        at Chichester Cathedral.

1985   Marc Chagall dies, 28th March.
* Dates stated are nominal and may vary from source to
source

Union Church Pocantico Hills, Tarrytown, New York, America

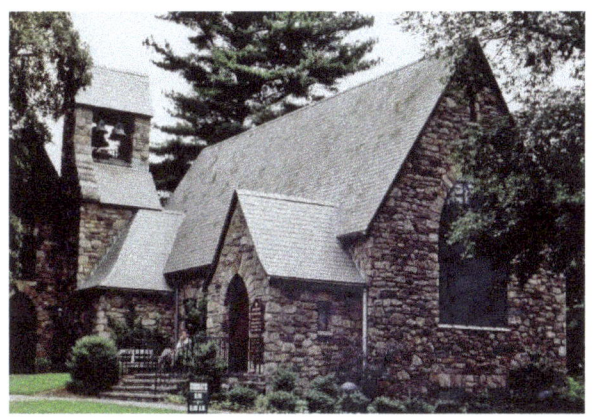

Union Church, Pocantico Hills

Approximately twenty miles north of New York city, New York, America, along the Hudson Valley, there is the district of Tarrytown. Here, the famous Rockefeller family have housed their estate. Less than a mile away from the estate is Pocantico Hills and the Union Church.

The church stands very close to a secondary road which runs through Pocantico Hills and therefore is at the centre of the community. Along the roadside sit large wooden and brick houses with immaculate lawns and gardens. Behind the building there is a large customised car park and beyond that vast banks of trees. The church building does not appear to have much age, with clean stone work walls and slate roof. The size of the meeting space is deceptive from the outside because of the added school rooms which are accessed by another entrance.

The church began life in 1880 as a Sunday school, which met in the schoolhouse on Wheeler Hill. Over the following years, the church grew to a thriving community which needed a larger building to meet in. By 1915, the formerly known Society for Christian Work became known as the Union Church of Pocantico Hills. The church continued to prosper and the desire for a new church building was often expressed. Finally, in 1922, the church building that we see today was completed after four years of planning under the architect L W Eisinger. The money was given by the congregation but vast gifts were also attributed by Mr Barron Collier, who would duplicate the giving of the congregation, Mr John D Rockefeller Sr. gave the most advantageous site for the building, and Mr John D Rockefeller Jr. donated the tower and chimes. Other donations towards the parish house and children's wing were also made.

On Mothers' Day in 1956 the memorial window to Abby Aldrich Rockefeller (Mrs John D Rockefeller Jr) a much loved mother and devoted worker in the church, was dedicated. The window was designed by Henri Matisse and was his last project. It was from this window that Chagall gained his inspiration. He wanted to single out the colours and relate his own work back to this window. [3]

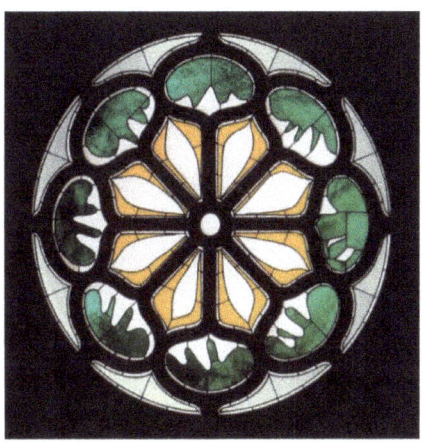

The Matisse Rose Window

The main entrance is approached by means of a short and wide flight of stairs. They are cut into the low mound upon which the church stands and introduce the passer-by to the church. The flagstone path leads in three directions; one down the side, another to the bell tower and the third to the entrance and then round the back of the building. The church is flanked by large trees on each of its faces marking the boundaries. The entrance is not obscured by the trees but is instead, inviting and welcoming with its small landscaped garden.

Again, there is a small rise of stairs leading you to three spaces. Here you can sit in a recess on lovely benches surrounded by shrubs with your back to two of the windows.

This space is relaxing and contemplative; however, it is unusual way to view the windows. The lead work can be seen but only glimpses of the stories the windows hold are caught, and that depends on the intensity of light that is flooding the interior and is shining through from the other side.

When you leave the building, this space offers an alternative purpose. Perhaps this is where you can sit when you have left, and begin to look inward after a visit to church and hearing the word of God. You may look for the meaning of the windows and their significance on your life.

This space could be used to clear your mind of whatever would hinder you upon entering and embarking on the spiritual journey.

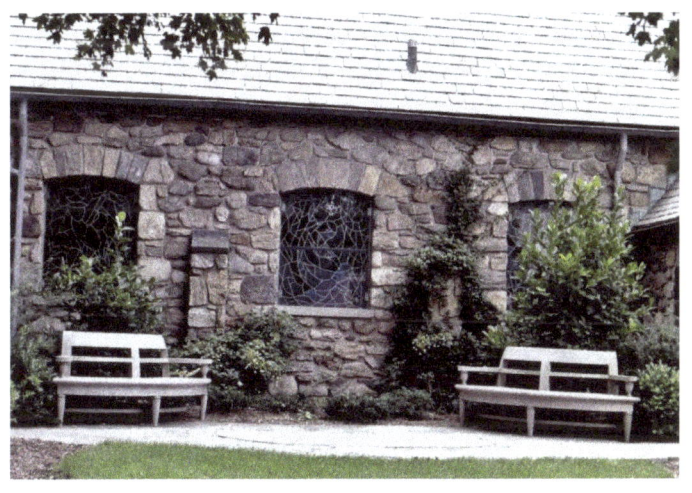

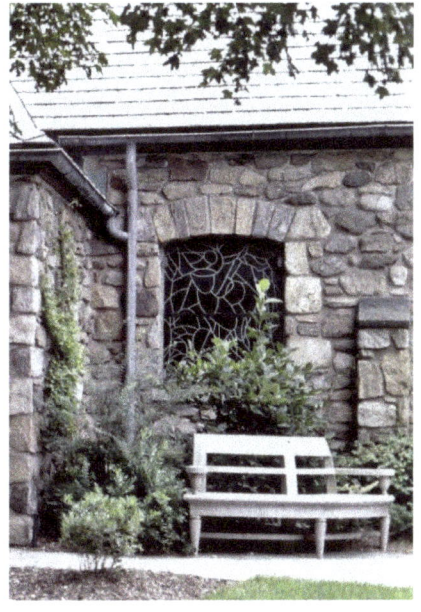

The recess, a place to sit

The porch is fully enclosed, therefore upon entering there is a real sense of crossing the threshold into the building. Many thresholds have already been crossed in terms of pathways and stairs, but none quite as strong as this. Not only are you coming from an expansive space, with its borders being the sky and ground to the enclosed space of the porch, but there is also a difference in the sound. Out in the open you can hear all sorts of daily activity. Inside it is hushed. Here the walls are so thick that they even deaden the sounds that the visitor makes. All the outside sounds are eradicated. The porch becomes the threshold.

Another door must be opened before entering the main space. The first thing you find as that door is opened is the sheer intensity of mingling colours. The air seems thick with them.

You are confronted to your right with the massive pictorial conception of the Good Samaritan by Marc Chagall. The depth and variation of the blues, in particular, capture your attention. It is only after you have absorbed some of this that you realise what space you are in.

The atmosphere is peaceful. The wooden flooring adds warmth to the space with its natural variations of grain. The pews are arranged with a carpet running down the central aisle. The walls are lightly textured which allows the beautiful light to be absorbed, causing them to possess an interior friendliness. This texture also encourages the light to bounce off into the atmosphere and touch you while within the space.

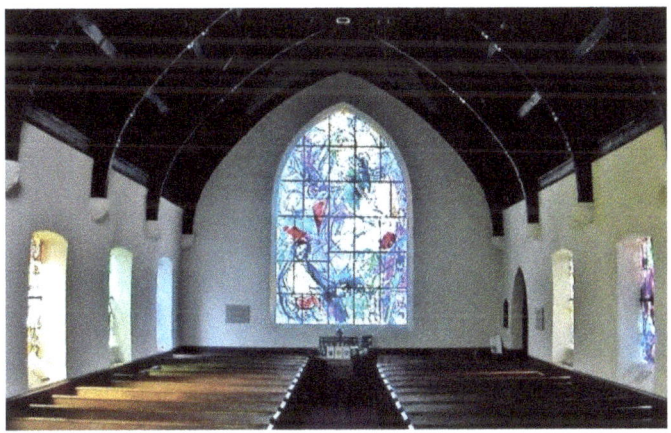

Union Church interior

In each of the four walls there is at least one example of an exquisite window. The longer walls of the rectangular space house four of the "Prophet" windows. At either end are the Matisse rose window, seen from the pews during a service, and the Good Samaritan at the rear of the room.

Dark wooden panelling runs around the room parallel with the bottom edge of the windows. The pitched ceiling is high and has dark wooden trusses and beams, but even the light seems to collect here. Electric spot lights now occupy this space for use when it is dark. Yet the space has a fantastic sense of natural light.

Although there are no physical boundaries within the space, the windows, and in particular, the Prophets create some inviting spiritual boundaries.

They offer to take you on a journey with their stories but also on a spiritual journey because of their pictorial stances, simple grace and touching light. Humility, prayer, adoration and praise are some of the attitudes that can be felt.

Chagall knew that people had a need not only to understand the stories, but go beyond them, to a place where they could find the right attitude towards God. He fulfilled this by use of a gentle journey where you could examine yourself by means of a sequence of windows, carefully positioned and not placed just by chance.

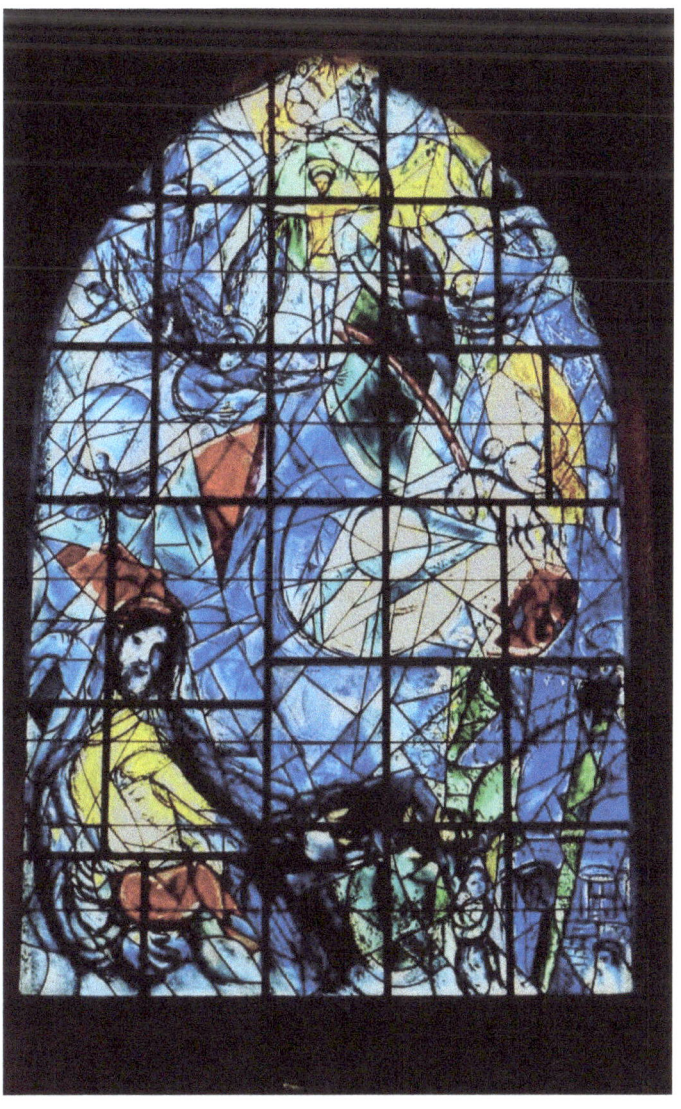

The Good Samaritan

The Good Samaritan

The Good Samaritan is a memorial window to John D Rockefeller Junior in the church in Pocantico Hills. This is how The Message tells the story of the Good Samaritan.

Jesus answered by telling a story. "There was once a man traveling from Jerusalem to Jericho. On the way he was attacked by robbers. They took his clothes, beat him up, and went off leaving him half-dead. Luckily, a priest was on his way down the same road, but when he saw him he angled across to the other side. Then a Levite religious man showed up; he also avoided the injured man.

"A Samaritan traveling the road came on him. When he saw the man's condition, his heart went out to him. He gave him first aid, disinfecting and bandaging his wounds. Then he lifted him onto his donkey, led him to an inn, and made him comfortable. In the morning he took out two silver coins and gave them to the innkeeper, saying, 'Take good care of him. If it costs any more, put it on my bill—I'll pay you on my way back.'
"What do you think? Which of the three became a neighbour to the man attacked by robbers?"

"The one who treated him kindly," the religion scholar responded.

Jesus said, "Go and do the same."

Luke 10:30-37 [4]

Chagall has portrayed the attack, the journey to the inn by donkey and the inn itself. He deliberately uses imagery that is not accurate.

The man has been ambushed by only one person, but it does give the feeling of loneliness and vulnerability by the large space that this scene occupies.

The next definite picture of the story is that of the Samaritan cradling the injured man on the donkey that looks just as gentle and caring as his master.

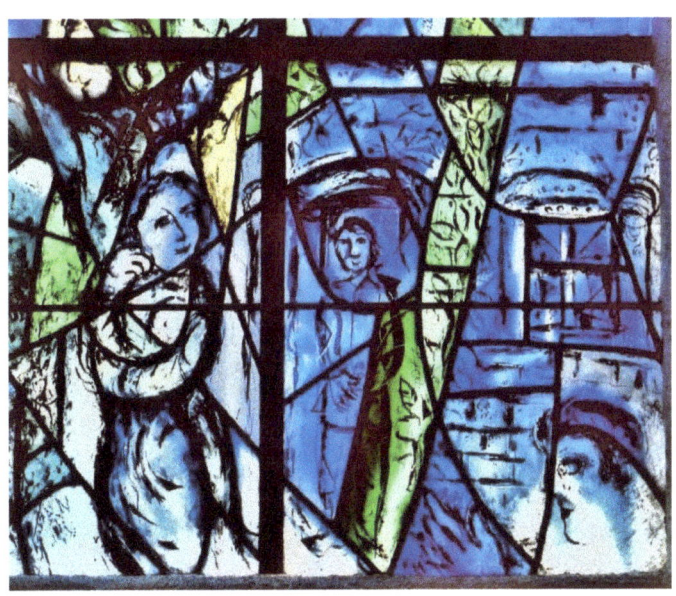

The western looking inn

Then there is the strange image of the inn. This looks more like a comfortable cottage than an inn in Israel. Chagall had visited Israel before and I expect had seen many photographs of his home land, so why paint such a western looking building? He used this imagery so that the local parishioners and visitors to the church would be able to understand the story that was told. He invited them to think about the story for application to their own lives. He did not want the barrier of unfamiliarity to alienate people from responding to his invitation into the story.

Other images flood the window too.

There is a thankful embrace. This, I think, is the man and the Samaritan. The use of a splash of red which is present in the two other scenes including the man almost makes this a certainty.

There is also a pose of Jesus on the cross. He is connected by a red streak to the man on the donkey and the Samaritan, with angels flying about him. To the right there is a dove.

Above this are two people, they may be the injured man being cared for by the Samaritan before being taken to the inn, or it may show the crucified Jesus being prepared before burial.

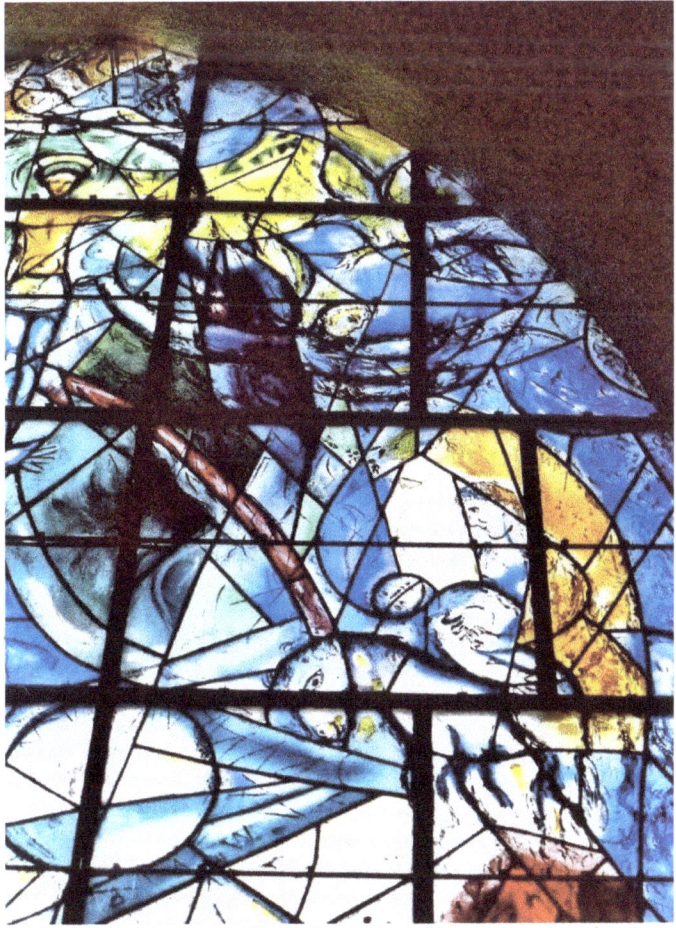

The Samaritan cradling the injured man on the donkey with the red streak connecting them to Jesus on the cross.

Beyond that there is a ladder which leads to the pinnacle of the window with someone climbing and two people in the background. These may be the people who did not help the man, or more convincingly be the image of ascending to heaven. The fact that this ladder is as high as it can go and that there are angels nearby, makes the latter a stronger option.

Chagall used the image of a ladder in some of his religious paintings; in these he also depicts heaven. The ladder image is probably taken from the dream that Jacob had in scripture.

At first glance there does seem to be two different story lines taking place in this window but Chagall would not do that. The two story lines would have a connection.

Jesus is the ultimate Good Samaritan. He went to his death to save the human race. However, is this what Chagall wanted to portray? Chagall was a Jew, so does he compromise his own beliefs of who Jesus is because this is a Christian place of worship? Chagall was not forced to paint what he painted. Many times Chagall painted Jesus on the cross and was not offended by it. He understood that the centre of the Christian belief is that of Jesus' death. He used this concept to provoke the congregation by placing it into the window.

The window reminds the viewer that The Good Samaritan died to common thinking that he should not help a Jew. They should have been enemies. This window challenges you to die to worldly thinking that says humans are of different race, religion and family. Jesus died for one and all, it is up to that person to accept or not.

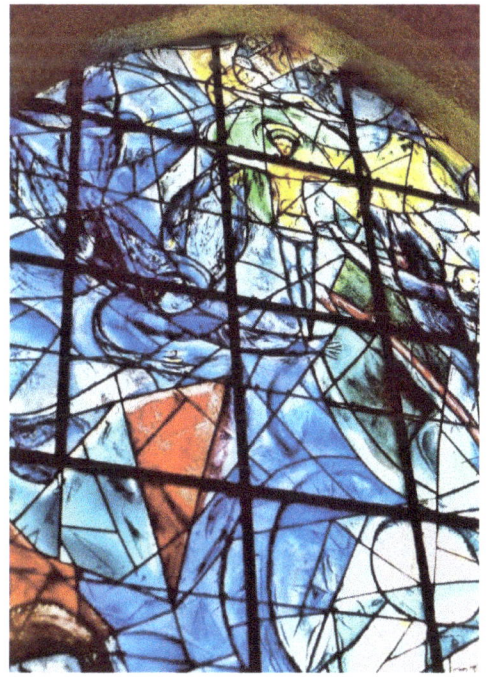

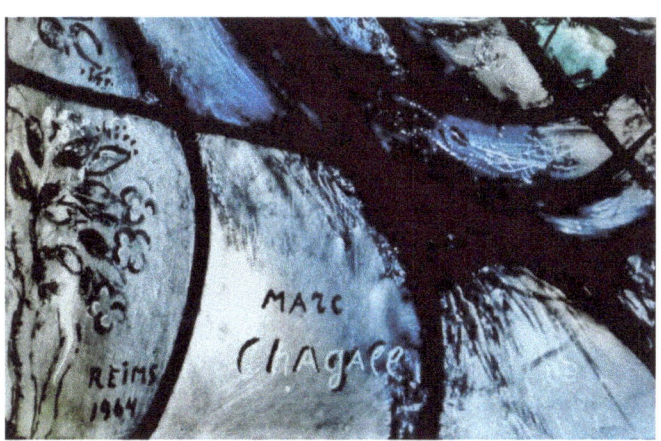

Details of The Good Samaritan

The Prophets in Union Church

Two years after the Good Samaritan was installed, eight more windows were completed. Six of the subjects were prophets of the Old Testament and the remaining two were The Crucifixion and Cherubim.

For me, painting the Bible is like a bouquet of flowers. The Bible for me is absolutely pure poetry, a human tragedy. The prophets inspire me, Jeremiah, Isaiah ... it is a committed poetry.[5]

The Prophet Joel

The day of the LORD
'And afterwards, I will pour out my Spirit on all people.
Your sons and daughters will prophesy, your old men
will dream dreams, your young men will see
visions. Even on my servants, both men and women, I
will pour out my Spirit in those days. I will show
wonders in the heavens and on the earth, blood and fire
and billows of smoke. The sun will be turned to
darkness and the moon to blood before the coming of
the great and dreadful day of the LORD.

Joel 2:28-31[6]

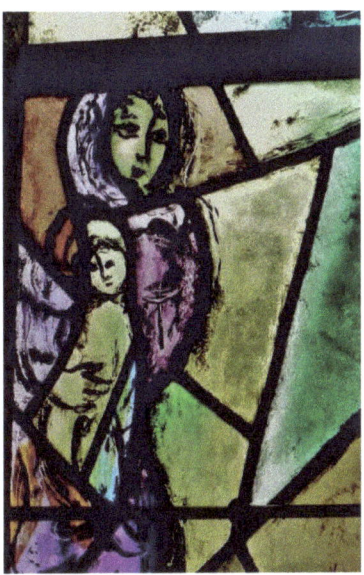

Detail of The Prophet Joel

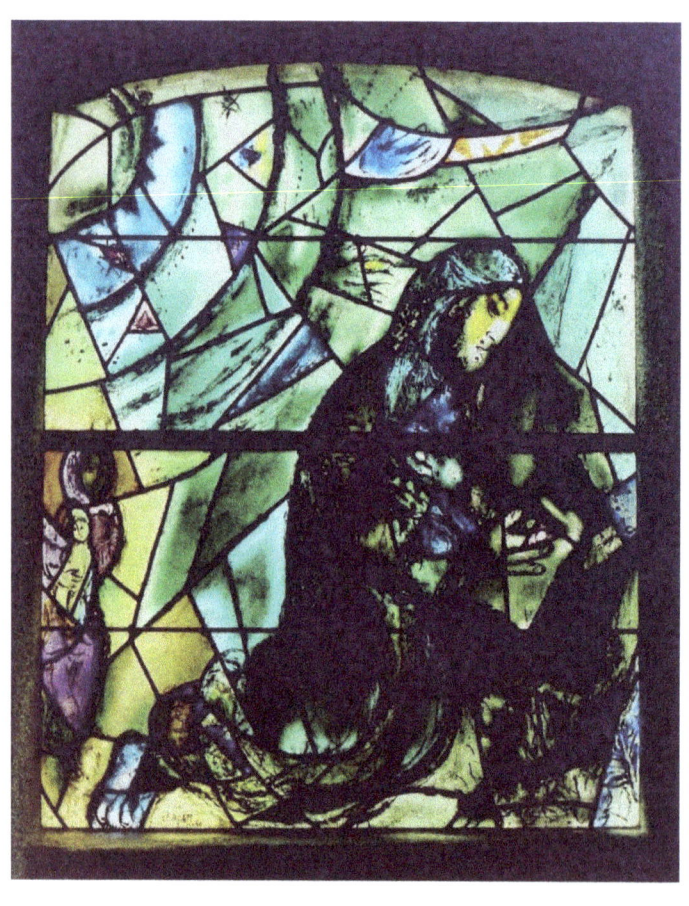

The Prophet Joel

Chagall used the image of hands in three of the Jerusalem windows of the tribes of Israel. In Judah the hands are said to be *outspread in benediction*[7], in Issachar the hands are the hands of blessing and the last is in Joseph. *Jacob's blessing says:*

"Joseph is a fruitful vine. A fruitful vine by a fountain, its branches run over the wall (he shall be widely blessed) ... With blessings of Heaven above."[8]

The hands in Joseph's window are the hands of God. They are depicted differently to that of the other tribes, his brothers. Therefore, in the window of Joel the hands are also the hands of God since the imagery is so similar. The use of colour here, also suggests that this is God.

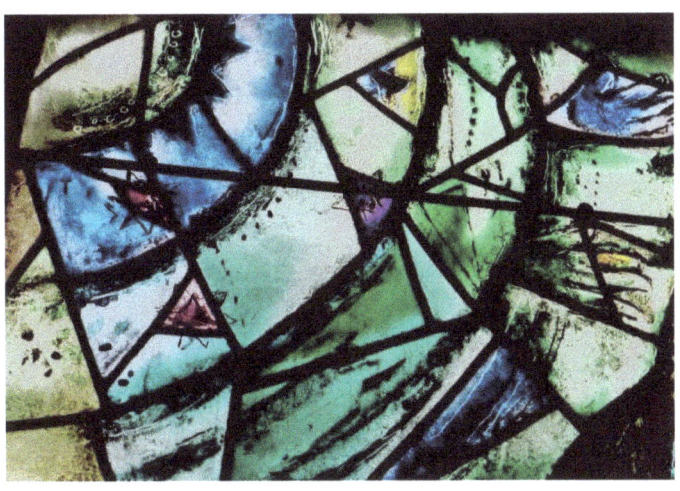

Detail of The Prophet Joel with "a rainbow resembling an emerald".

The use of colour in The Prophet Joel, also suggests that this is God. In Revelation 4:2-3 and 4:10-11a it says:

There before me was a throne in heaven with someone sitting on it. And the one who sat there had the appearance of jasper and carnelian. A rainbow, resembling an emerald, encircled the throne.

The twenty four elders fall down before him who sits on the throne, and worship him who lives forever. They lay down their crowns before the throne and say,
"You are worthy, our Lord and God, to receive glory and honour and power."

These hands are the hands of God inspiring Joel to prophesy about the events in Acts 2:17-21 and 39. Joel kneels and writes down the things that God tells him. Kneeling is a sign of humility. Joel could also be kneeling in awe as the realisation of what the prophecy means to mankind.

Behind him there is a woman and child. These people could be those who fulfil the prophecy Joel was given, but they are likely to be Mary and Jesus by their traditional stance and appearance. For in order for this prophecy to happen God needed to send his son Jesus. He would need to die, rise again and ascend into heaven, for the Holy Spirit to be left with those who believed. Joel could be contemplating such wonders, so that the dreams and visions could happen.

The Prophet Elijah

When they had crossed, Elijah said to Elisha, "Tell me what I can do for you before I am taken from you?"

"Let me inherit a double portion of your spirit Elijah's replied.

"You have asked for a difficult thing," Elijah said, "yet if you see me when I am taken from you, it will be yours – otherwise not."

As they were walking along and talking together, suddenly a chariot of fire appeared and separated the two of them, and Elijah went up into heaven in a whirlwind. Elisha saw this and cried out, "My father! My father! The chariot and horsemen of Israel!" And Elisha saw him no more. Then he took hold of his clothes and tore them apart.

2 Kings 2:9-12

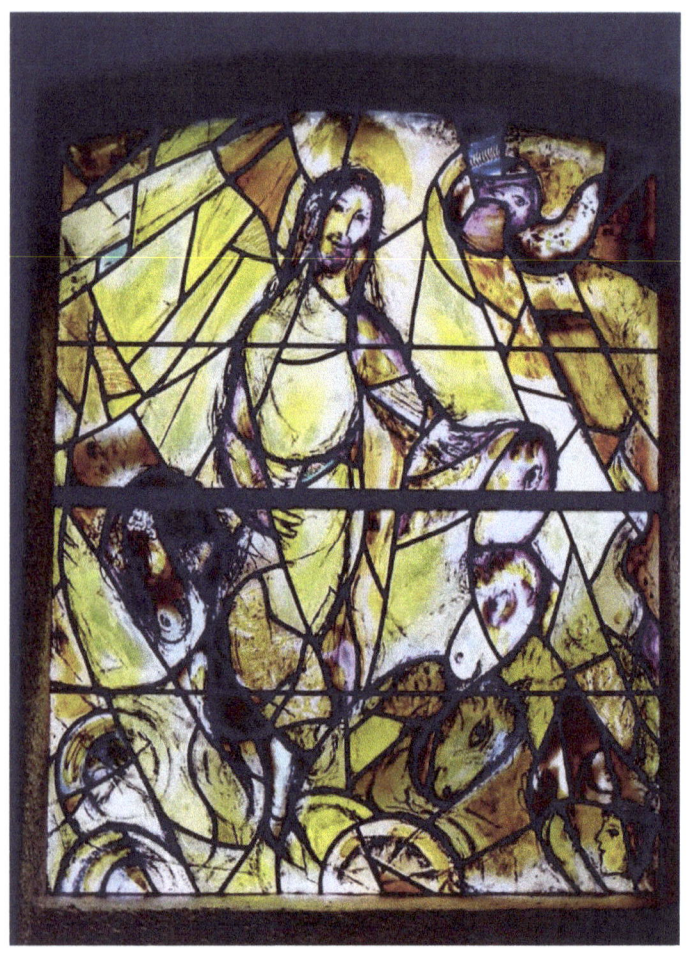

The Prophet Elijah

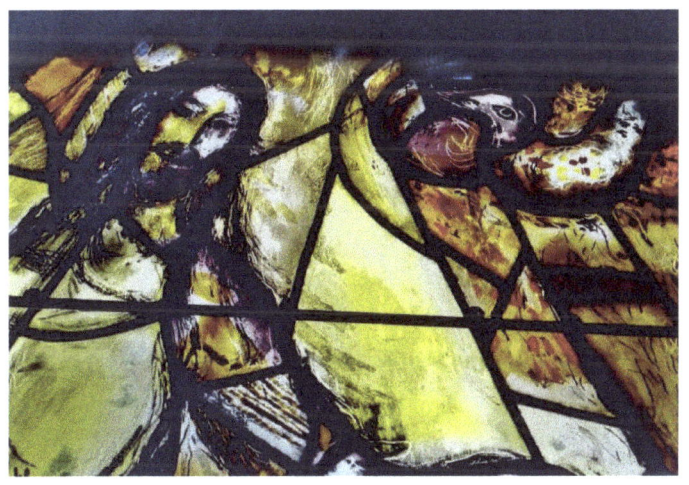

Details of The Prophet Elijah

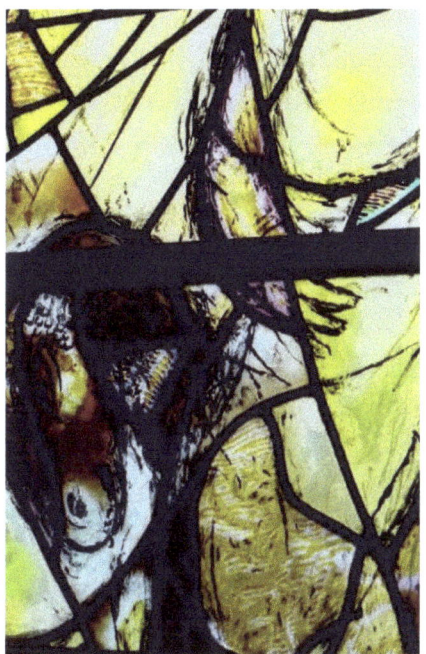

Chagall shows Elijah being taken from Elisha who is looking on. Elijah is surrounded by horses and chariot wheels and the glass is leaded as if he is being drawn up in shafts of light. Elisha almost waves goodbye in the bottom right corner. Above him is a bird which can be closely related to many of Chagall's depictions of doves. Chagall may be trying to suggest the transferring of the double portion of Elijah's spirit onto Elisha by this symbolism. Christians know that it was the Holy Spirit that descended on Jesus in bodily form like a dove, therefore they can relate to it.

This depiction is full of energy and excitement. The viewer is caught up in the chariot and the horses are animated.

Considering the underlying sombre tones of this account, Chagall has definitely focused on the joyous hope that the story also brings; the hope for Elisha to do great things under the double portion blessing. It is no longer a depressing farewell but focuses the people of Israel on God, his power and his prophet.

The Prophet Daniel

While I, Daniel, was watching the vision and trying to understand it, there before me stood one who looked like a man. And I heard a man's voice from the Ulai calling, 'Gabriel, tell this man the meaning of the vision.'

As he came near the place where I was standing, I was terrified and fell prostrate. 'Son of man,' he said to me, 'understand that the vision concerns the time of the end.'

While he was speaking to me, I was in a deep sleep, with my face to the ground. Then he touched me and raised me to my feet.

Daniel 8:15-18

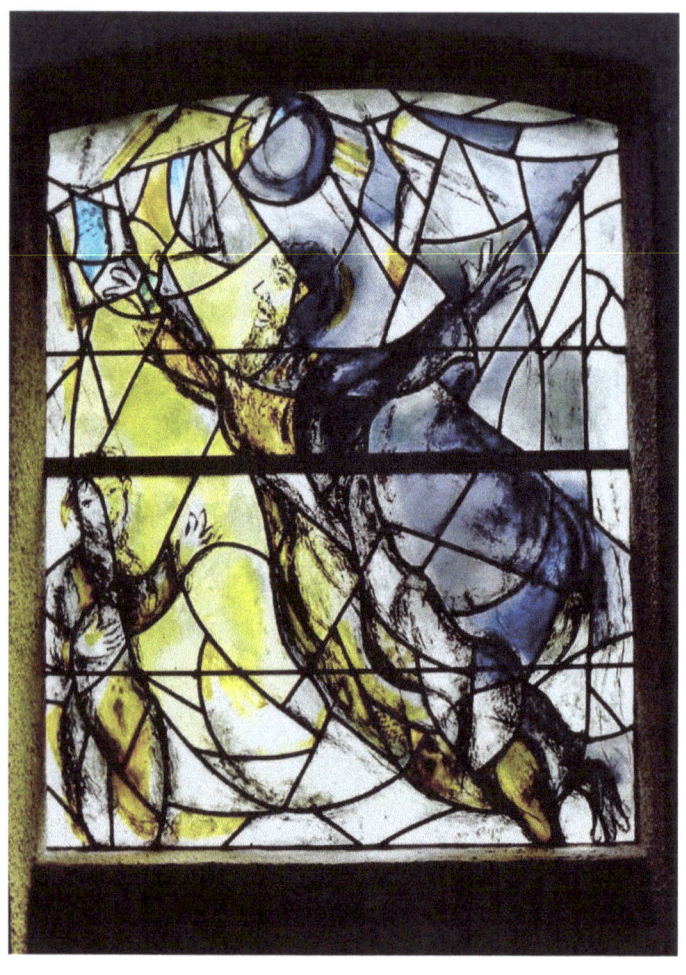

The Prophet Daniel

Daniel stretches diagonally through this window with a man in the bottom left corner reaching out to him but looking at the viewer.

The man in the background is suggested by the text to be the angel Gabriel yet this image is not like Chagall's other depictions of angels. The text refers to one who looked like a man.

Daniel could be shown as falling down to worship just as Ezekiel had done at the revelation of God's glory (Ezekiel 3:23), or being raised up by the touch of Gabriel. He is looking up at a book in his right hand.

As for the reason for the book's presence, there could be a couple of explanations. When Chagall depicts the prophets that have a book in the Bible named after them he usually includes the symbol of a book. However, one of the stained glass prophets, Isaiah, does have a book in the Bible named after him but a book does not appear in the window.

The absence of the book in Isaiah's window and the presence of the book here must symbolise something else, namely the impartation of the word of God to Daniel.

The colours in this window are not as vibrant as in other windows. Chagall mostly uses the white light that pours through the clear glass and his detailing work to translate the message. The other windows have vitality to them and could stand strong just with their use of colour. Here the colour is focused in small areas.

Chagall understood colours, and there is evidence of that all the way round the building, so why should he use such a lack of colours here? This window is closest to the altar on the right hand wall. Chagall is removing distraction for the congregation by removing the vast array of colours.

Chagall wanted this window to have a relationship to the Matisse window above the altar. On the right hand side of the church as you enter you can see that the primary colour used in the four windows relate directly to the Matisse rose window, using blue (Crucifixion), green (Joel), yellow (Elijah) and white or black (Daniel).

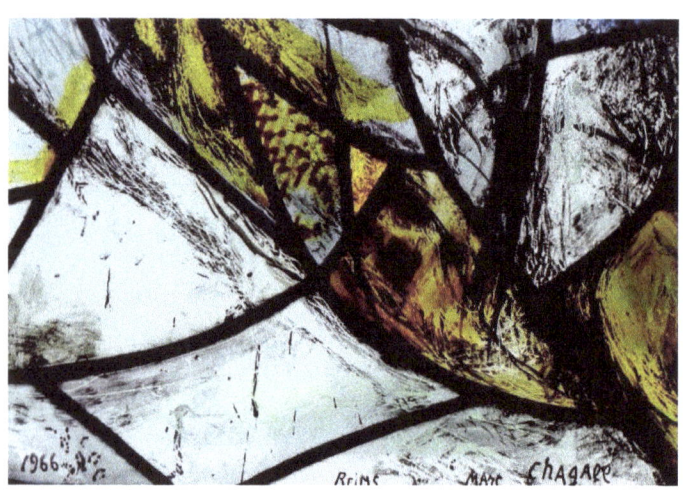

Detail of The Prophet Daniel

The Crucifixion

Ask and it will be given to you; seek and you will find; knock and the door will be opened to you.

Matthew 7:7

This window is a memorial to Michael Clark Rockefeller who died in New Guinea. His brother, Steven, suggested the quotation and asked for an image of Christ to be used among the Old Testament subjects so that *the meaning of life through the example and teaching of Christ* [6] may be told.

The window shows Jesus on the cross with a man humbly kneeling before him. The man's humility is also expressed by the hand being placed on his chest.

An angel bends down to speak to the man who looks like he is receiving revelation.

A bird, most probably a dove which represents the Holy Spirit, is just above the head of Christ.

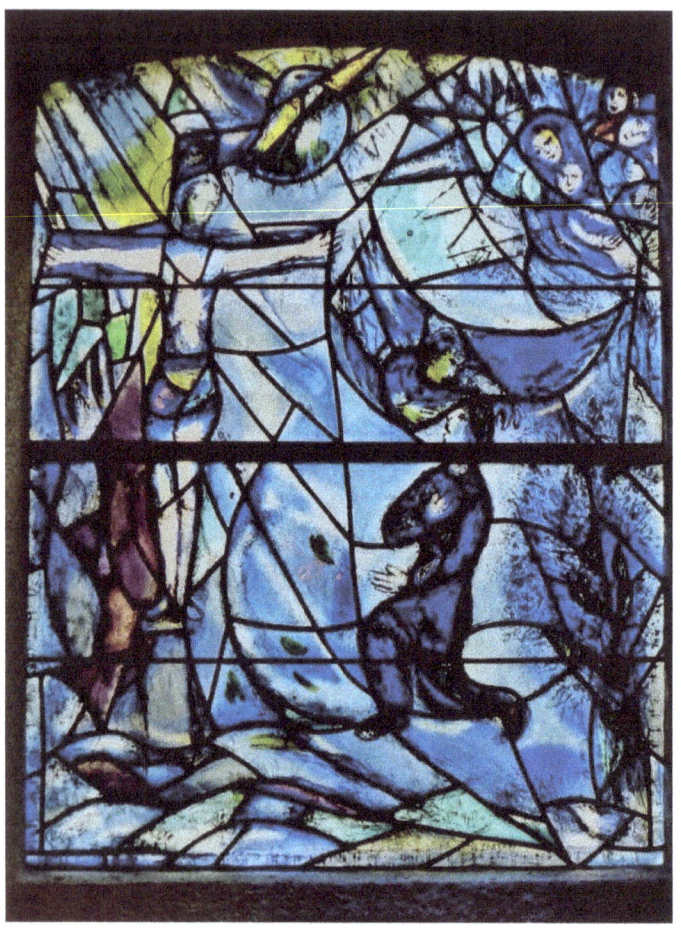

The Crucifixion

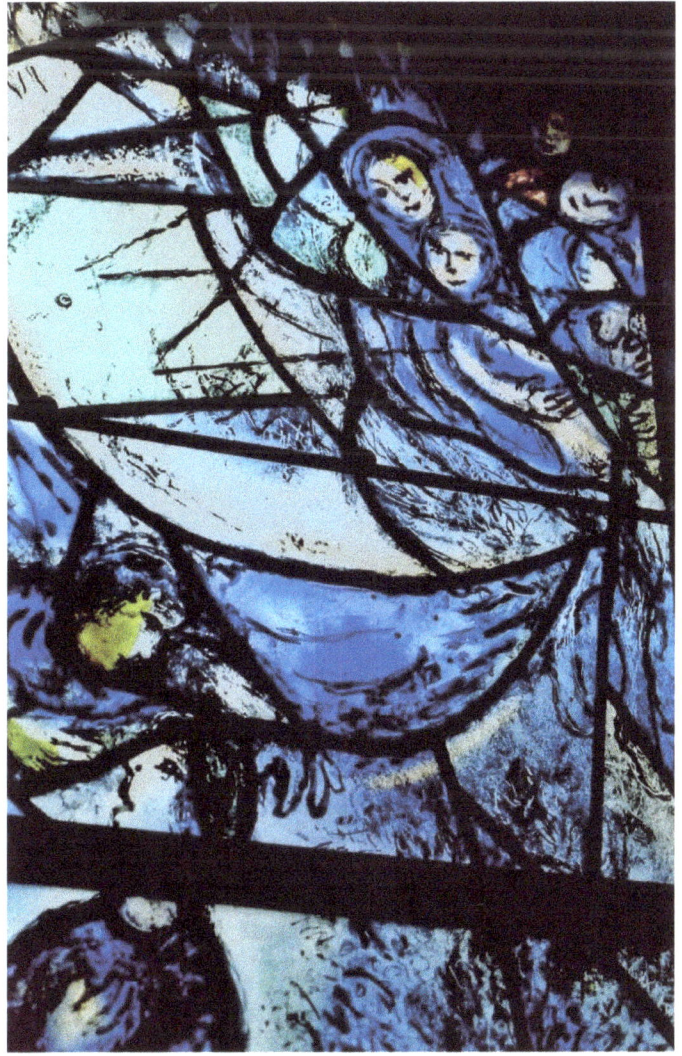

Detail of The Crucifixion

In the top right corner there are many onlookers. These people appear to be peering down from heaven, expressed by the shafts of light that surround them. For that would be a sombre moment, these people are very happy. Their joy is found because the man kneeling has discovered the meaning of life that Steven Rockefeller wanted this window to reveal.

A memorial window reminds the viewer of a life lived and a death. The subject of this window expresses the hope of eternal life in heaven for those that receive God. The revelation that the angel speaks of is that of Jesus' life laid down in sacrifice for others.

The red and purple flowing from the side of Jesus suggests the blood poured out, and even pooling on the ground at the foot of the cross.

The plant on the right hand side could symbolise the promised new life received by the man worshipping at the cross.

The Prophet Ezekiel

But you, son of man, listen to what I say to you. Do not rebel like that rebellious people; open your mouth and eat what I give you.'

Then I looked, and I saw a hand stretched out to me. In it was a scroll, which he unrolled before me. On both sides of it were written words of lament and mourning and woe.
And he said to me, 'Son of man, eat what is before you, eat this scroll; then go and speak to the people of Israel.'
So I opened my mouth, and he gave me the scroll to eat.

Then he said to me, 'Son of man, eat this scroll I am giving you and fill your stomach with it.' So I ate it, and it tasted as sweet as honey in my mouth.

Ezekiel 2:8-3:3

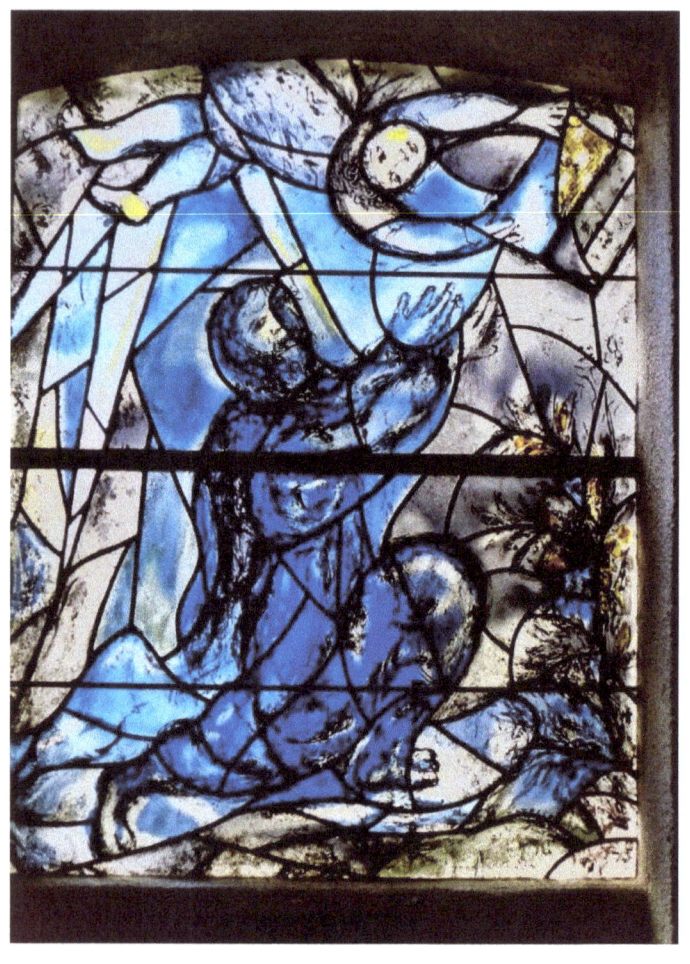

The Prophet Ezekiel

An angelic being holds the scroll or book above the head of Ezekiel, and Ezekiel reaches up to take it. The angel, however, does not look willing to part with it yet. This pausing helps us to understand that Ezekiel was asked three times to eat the scroll before he ate it. The window expresses the eagerness and urgency that Ezekiel finally had in his heart to then do what God had commanded. This highlights the importance of doing things in God's timing.

Chagall used an unusual technique to sign this window. He rubbed his name into the grisaille leaving a dark edge. On other windows he used dark paint to sign his name.

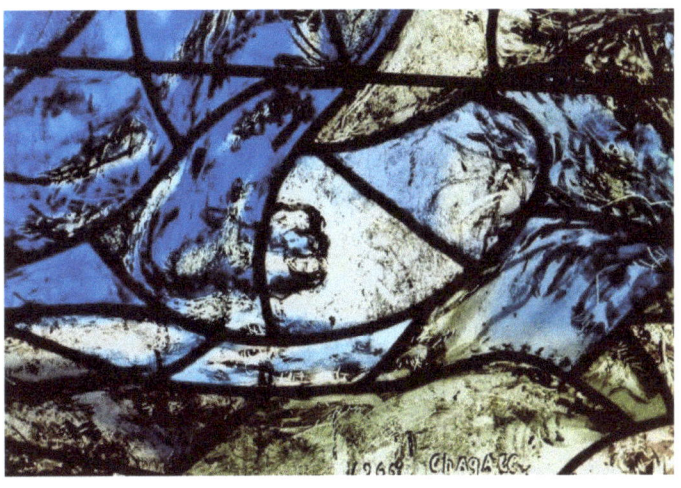

Detail of The Prophet Ezekiel

The Prophet Jeremiah

I am the man who has seen affliction
*   by the rod of the LORD's wrath.*
He has driven me away and made me walk
*   in darkness rather than light; indeed, he has turned*
his hand against me
*   again and again, all day long.*
He has made my skin and my flesh grow old
*   and has broken my bones.*
He has besieged me and surrounded me
*   with bitterness and hardship.*
He has made me dwell in darkness
*   like those long dead.*
He has walled me in so that I cannot escape;
*   he has weighed me down with chains.*
Even when I call out or cry for help,
*   he shuts out my prayer.*
He has barred my way with blocks of stone;
*   he has made my paths crooked.*

Lamentations 3:1-9

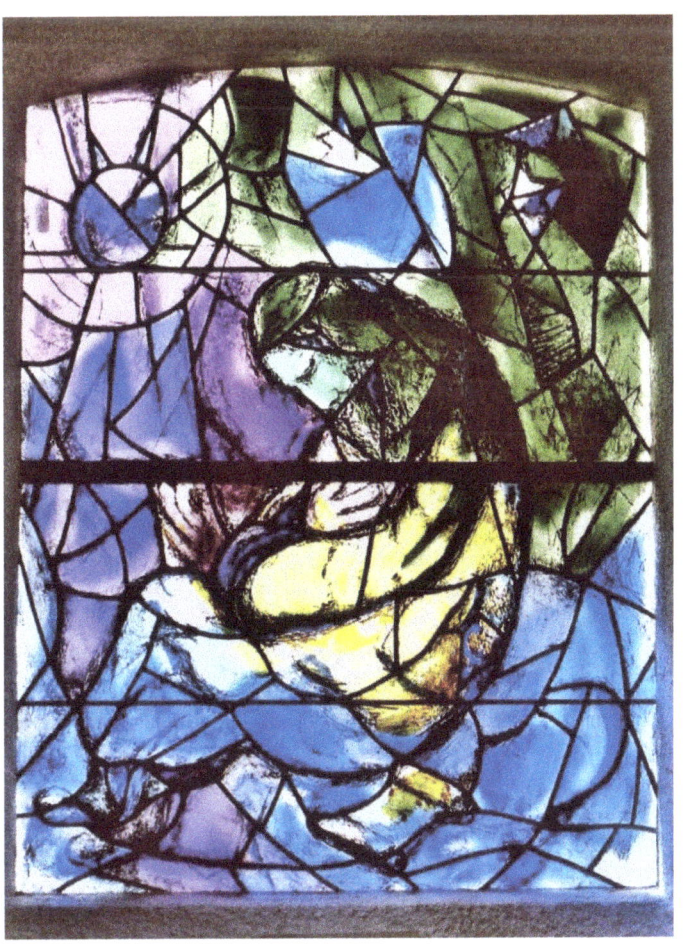

The Prophet Jeremiah

Jeremiah was appointed by God to be a prophet to the nations (Jeremiah 1:4-5).

Here we see Jeremiah dwelling in darkness. Perhaps Chagall was suggesting the darkness that his nation was still facing even after all this time and even a realisation that all nations were in darkness and in need of a word from God.

Chagall shows the stars and the moon, a form of darkness. He has his hand on his heart and his head is bowed with his eyes shut. This may be seen as resting by some but Jeremiah is waiting to hear God, he is in an attitude of worship. The positioning of the untouched scroll on the floor next to him shows that he is fully concentrated on waiting on God.

The colours in this window in particular are extremely vivid and include the whole range of the spectrum. The golden torso focuses the viewer on the attitude of Jeremiah, almost emphasising the heartfelt worship that he has towards God.

The text that accompanies this window talks of bitterness, hardship and finding no favour with God. It describes loneliness and sorrow. The window expresses all of this. This image is the most moving in the church.

There are times in life when as humans, we feel as if the odds are stacked against us. This is the situation that Jeremiah finds himself in. However, it is the peace that this image communicates that teaches us of the attitude of a man after God's heart. This is a man who would not allow the world to affect his spiritual life. It is by Jeremiah's attitude that we will learn to wait on God and find favour with him.

A quote often taken from Jeremiah is found in chapter 29 and verse 11.

For I know the plans I have for you,' declares the LORD, 'plans to prosper you and not to harm you, plans to give you hope and a future.

If I apply this verse to mind when viewing this window, Jeremiah bows in awe at the God who cares enough to plan the days of his life. A new life can be breathed into this window when expressed as hope and not bitterness. In fact, Jeremiah looks to be almost smiling as if he has received the revelation that God has it all in his almighty hands.

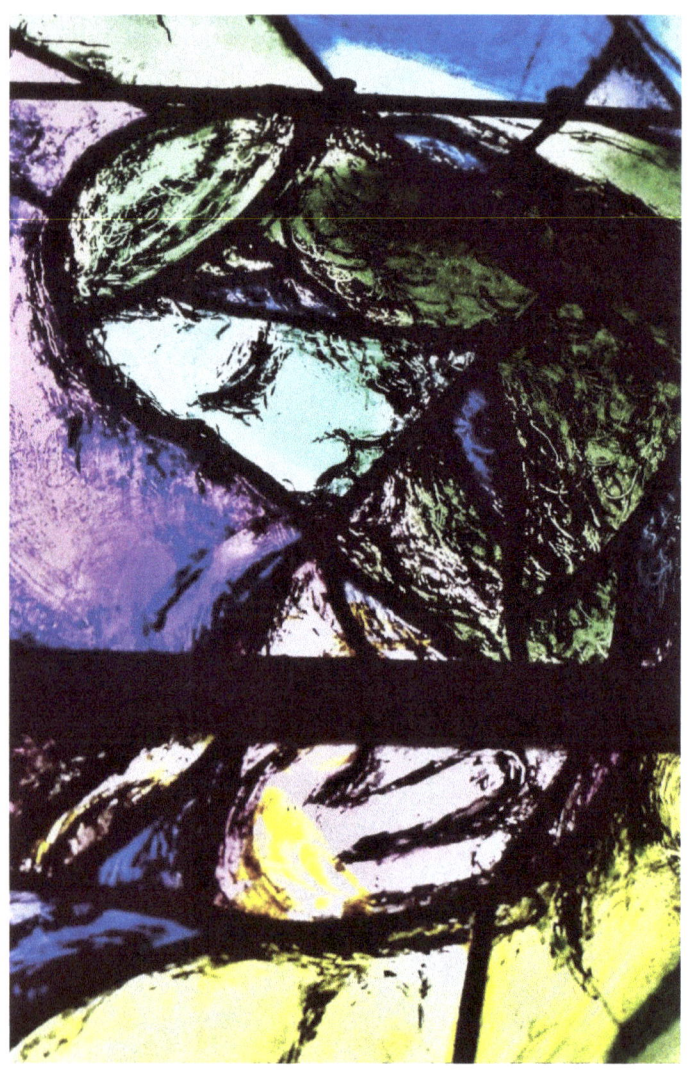

Detail of the Prophet Jeremiah

The Prophet Isaiah

All of us have become like one who is unclean,
      and all our righteous acts are like filthy rags;
we all shrivel up like a leaf,
      and like the wind our sins sweep us away.
No one calls on your name
      or strives to lay hold of you;
for you have hidden your face from us
      and have given us over to our sins.
Yet you, LORD, are our Father.
      We are the clay, you are the potter;
      we are all the work of your hand.
Do not be angry beyond measure, LORD;
      do not remember our sins for ever.
Oh, look upon us we pray,
      for we are all your people.
Your sacred cities have become a wasteland;
      even Zion is a wasteland, Jerusalem a desolation.
Our holy and glorious temple, where our ancestors
praised you,
      has been burned with fire,
      and all that we treasured lies in ruins.

Isaiah 64:6-11

This is the text that is given to the window of Isaiah. However, when the window was dedicated the sponsors of the tribute to the Walkers chose the following.

'As for me, this is my covenant with them,' says the LORD. 'My Spirit, who is on you, will not depart from you, and my words that I have put in your mouth will always be on your lips, on the lips of your children and on the lips of their descendants – from this time on and for ever,' says the LORD.

Isaiah 59:21

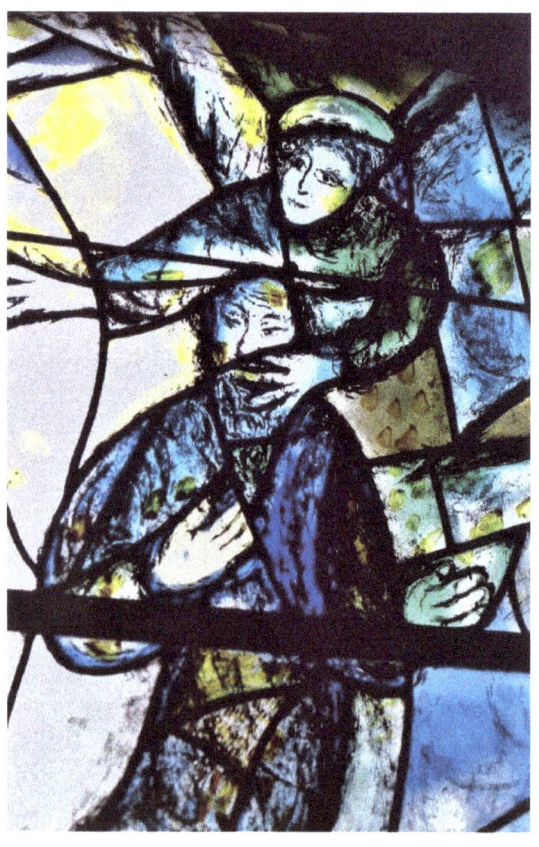

The Prophet Isaiah

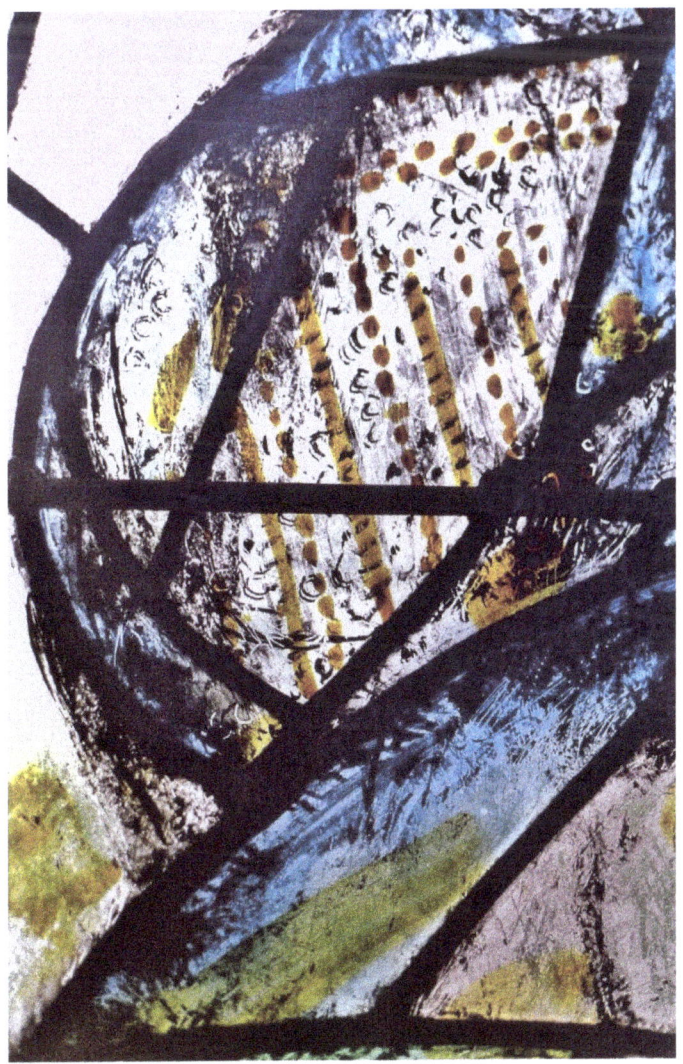

Details of The Prophet Isaiah

As with Joel, Jeremiah and the man at the foot of the cross, Isaiah has his hand on his heart. All of these four windows have a subject in common; they are all depictions of listening to God. The other prophets are involved in actions; Chagall had used this posture as a sign of listening. Therefore the second scripture reference describes the window more successfully.

An angel holds the mouth of Isaiah either to stop him from talking or as it states in the scripture, to place the words into his mouth, to listen to what God has to say. This imagery is quite humorous. For in order for us to hear anything, we must first stop speaking ourselves.

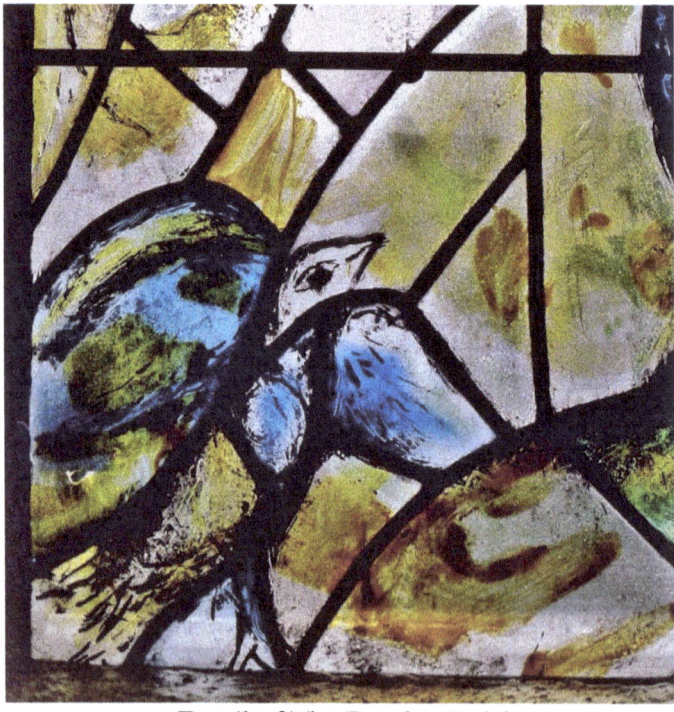

Detail of The Prophet Isaiah

Other angels above Isaiah are also showing him a vision. The angel holding his mouth looks intently at the vision and is physically guiding Isaiah towards it. He is taking him to a place where he can receive.

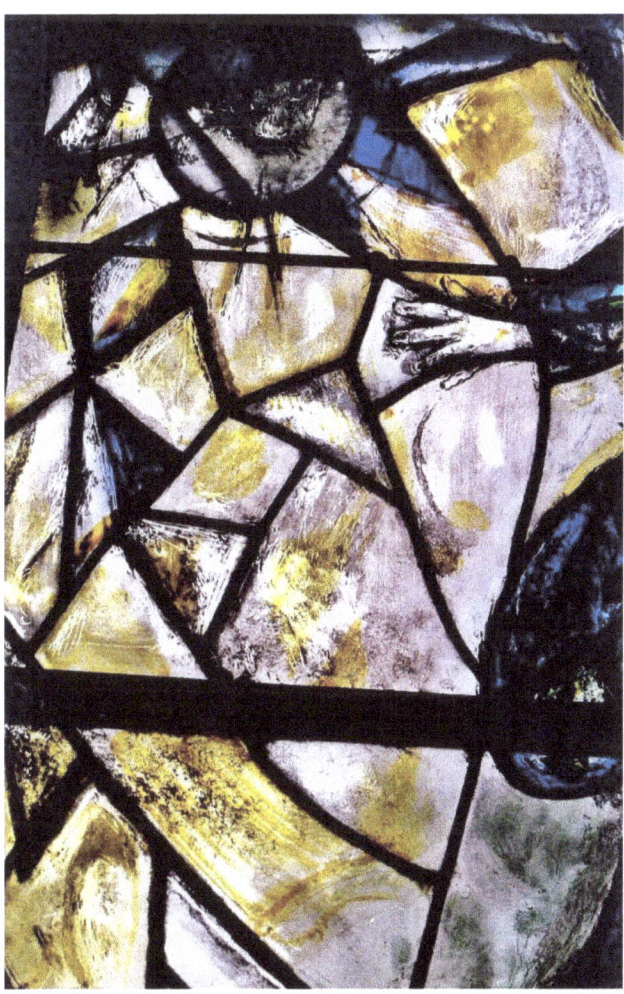

Detail of The Prophet Isaiah – the disclosing of the vision

Cherubim

After he drove the man out, he placed on the east side of the Garden of Eden cherubim and a flaming sword flashing back and forth to guard the way to the tree of life.

Genesis 3:24

The main characters in this window are the angels. Chagall has used many different colours and textures which altogether make an amazing flash of activity. Each pane of glass could in itself be used to exhibit, the joint effect is outstanding.

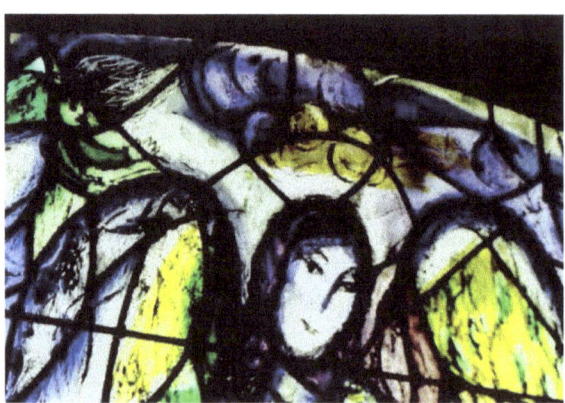

The window attempts to reflect the beauty of God's perfect creation before the fall of man in the details of the wings and garments of the main angel or cherubim.

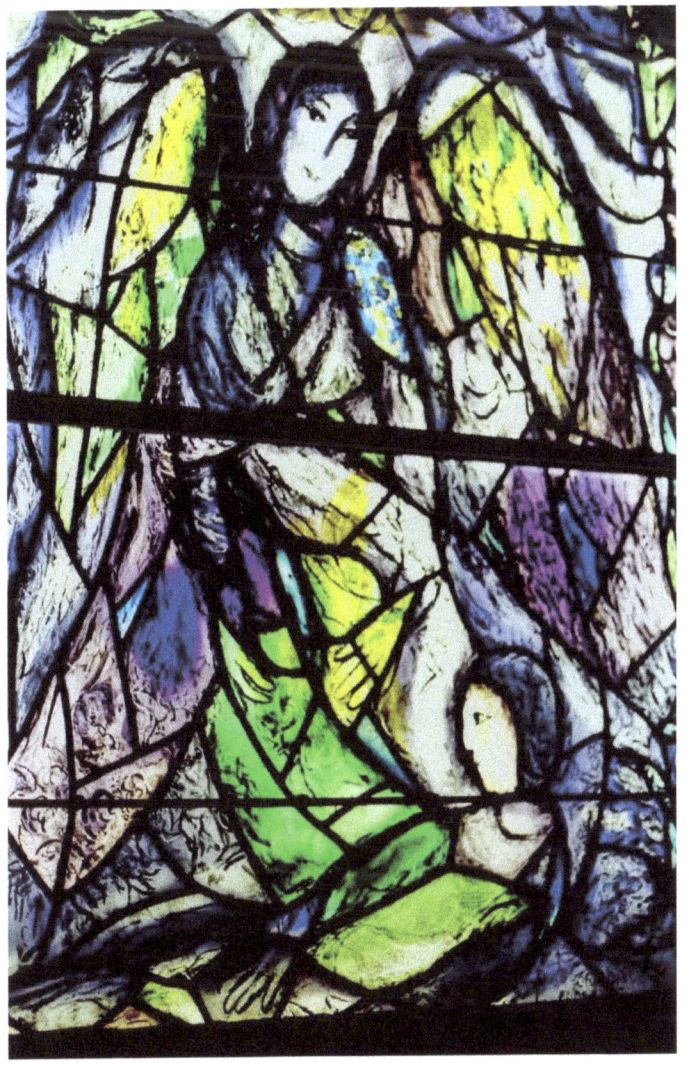

The Cherubim

As a secondary focus, there are Adam and Eve with the image of Christ, arms outstretched behind them. It was because of Adam and Eve's sin or fall that there was a need for God to send Jesus to die. Chagall knew that this is a fundamental belief for Christians, so again abandoned his birth religion of Judaism, to bring the real meaning to the people who would view this window as part of the church.

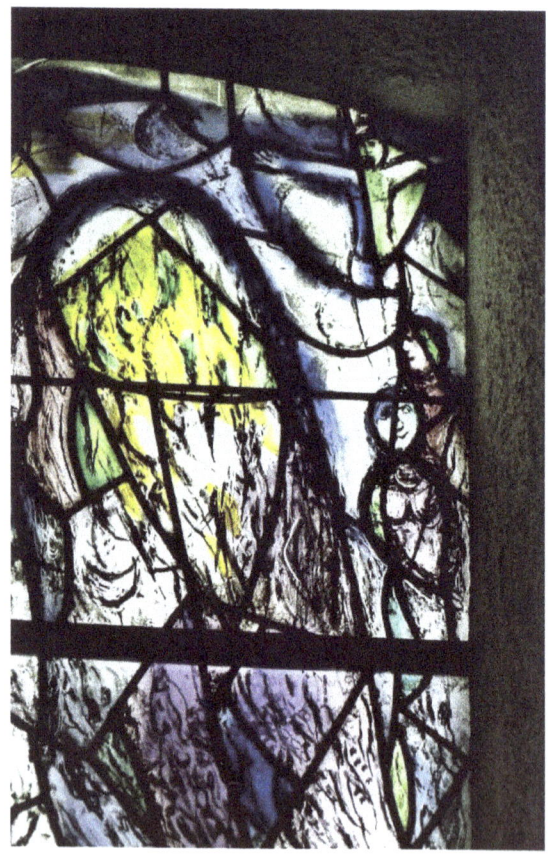

Detail of The Cherubim

All Saints Church
Tudeley,
Kent,
England

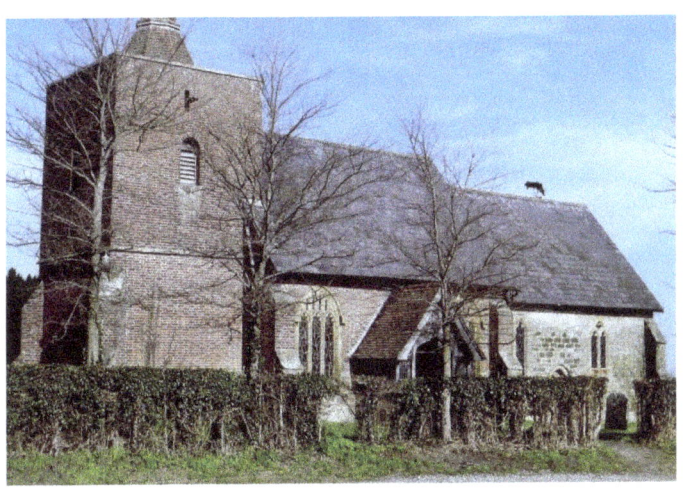

All Saints Church, Tudeley

Near Tonbridge in Kent, there lies a small community in the village of Tudeley. When this community was young, a church, then the centre of life, was built. It was positioned along the dirt tracks and bridle paths so that both parishioners and travellers had easy access. These days, the church stands a few metres from a secondary road and has seen many changes.

The most recent change has been to its glass windows. Following the tragic death of their daughter in a sailing accident, Sir Henry and Lady D'avigdor Goldsmid commissioned Marc Chagall to design the large window space in the east wall. Later the rest of the windows in this chapel were designed by Chagall and crafted by Charles Marq.

The beauty of these windows reflects the emotions of worshipping God. The quality of this space has been transformed by the installation of these windows. The restoration the church went through to accommodate them and the sheer uniqueness of their design makes the viewer stand back and reassess their view of stained glass. These are not traditional peices, but inspired.

As you approach the church through the small graveyard, you come to the porch. Even though you are covered and because you are not enclosed, there is neither a feeling of entering or staying outside. The porch was designed and built before the church was restored and the windows ever conceived. It seems to disturb the dramatic hard line boundary that could have easily have been formed from the heavy stone exterior to the interior.

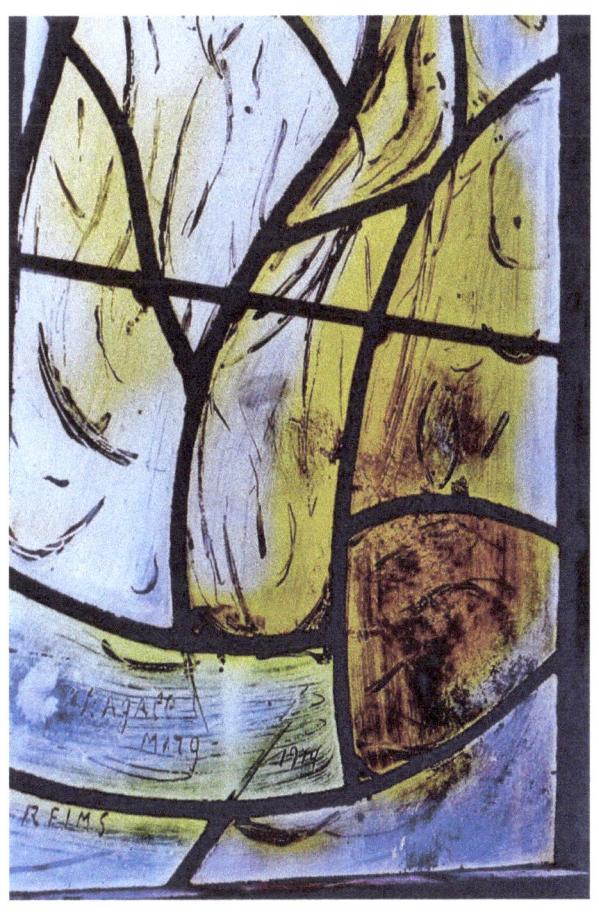

Detail of an abstract window

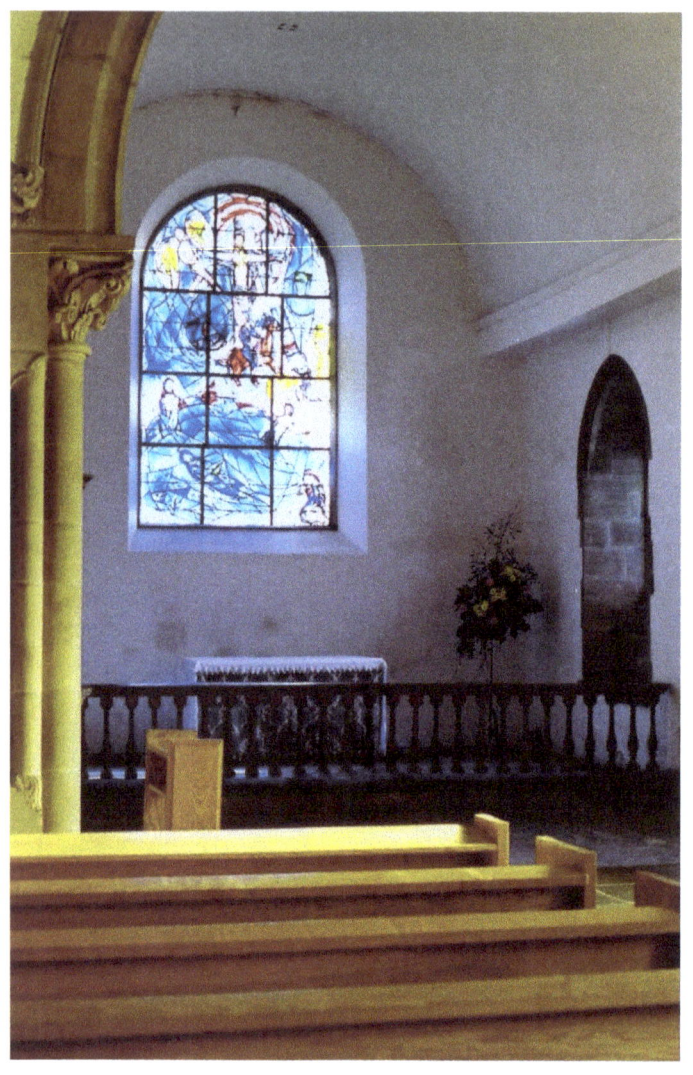

The East Window

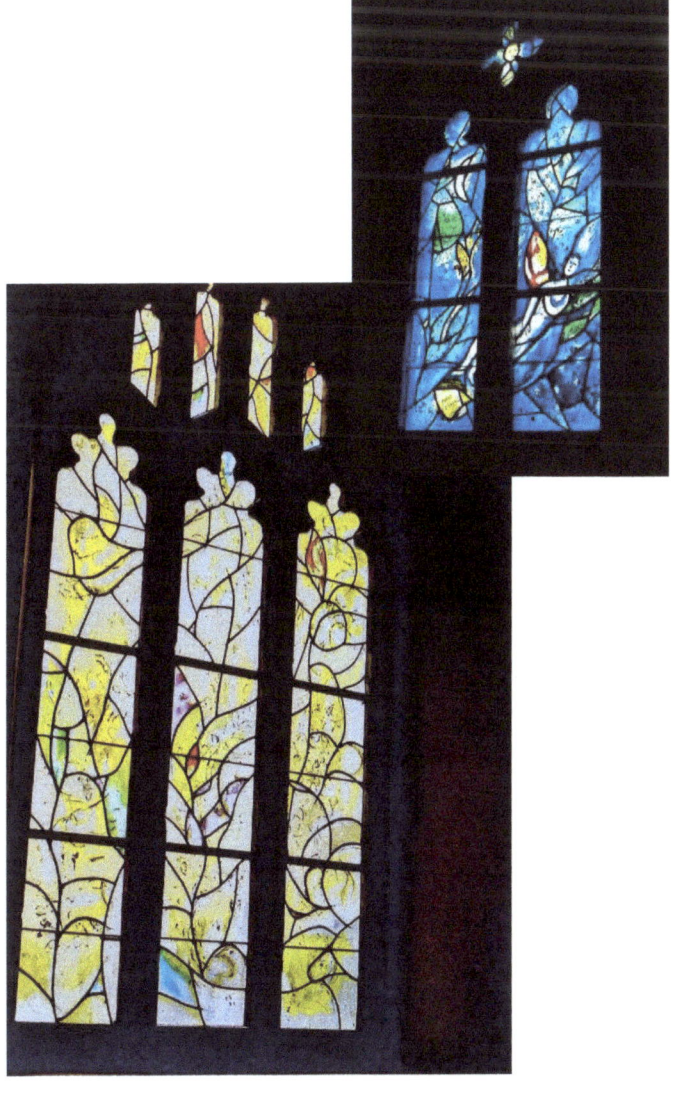

Abstract windows – the change of temperature by the use of colour

The old fashioned and authentic solid oak door creates a barrier that is easy to overcome, but is one that leads you to a different world. As soon as you cross the threshold you are bathed in an amazing intensity of light. Outside the light is crisp and clear, but inside it has a remarkable depth to it.

The windows either side of the door are predominately yellow, but when you enter you cannot see them, but you can feel the warmth of their colour covering you. This happy and welcoming colour gives the church building the feeling as if it has shaken you by the hand or welcomed you with a kiss. The flagstones on the floor, you know are cold and hard, but the reflections and paths of light make you to dismiss what you really know. The flagstones become warm and soft.

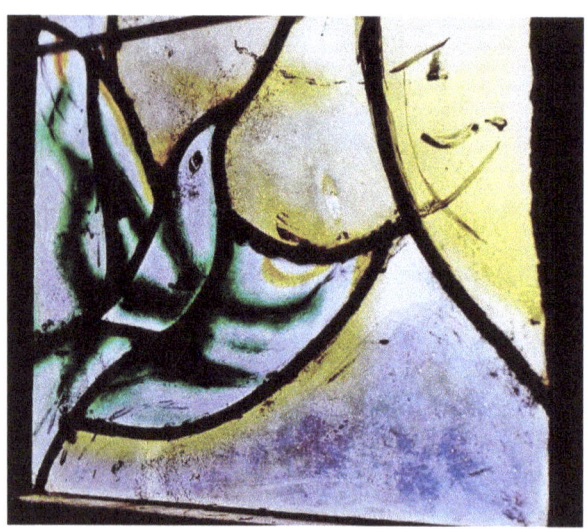

Detail of a yellow abstract window

Opposite the transept an edge is formed by the distinctive blue light. This edge or barrier is defined by the change of colour of light, but also has a very dramatic change of temperature. These two areas, the entrance and the transept are separated by gothic arches, so there is a physical barrier, but if the windows and light in both areas were the same in colour the barrier would almost be lifted. However, the contrast of bright, energetic yellow against the more passive blue, creates the feel of temperature change and a tension is formed .It is both the physical barrier of the arches and the change in the colour of light that separates the spaces. They do not outweigh each other at all but instead they are complimentary. The reflections and light of these opposites mingle on the flagstones and in the air. Therefore, sometimes there seems no edge at all.

These blue windows, when approached have their own compartment, their own space, which is introduced to the church building and you by the arches. The gothic arches express a worshipping pose and the privacy of this space, with the help of the colours, cause the heart to reflect and to worship. In this space, the covering has quite low wooden slats which, because of the scale of this area, humble and focus you on the reason for coming into the church.

The ceiling covering the congregation is curved green veined marble. Here the height is at its maximum. When elements of this area, the yellow light from one side, the blue form the other and the climax of the ceiling are put together, the attitude of the congregation should be one of praise, adoration and worship to God.

Tudeley's abstract windows around the church are full of suggestions. *There are suggestions of foliage and flowers, and all are rich in Chagall's personal brand of birds and beasts. There is even an angel touchingly inscribed Vava, the name of his second wife.*[10] Even though there may not be any definite images, the windows work wonderfully in the space. The abstract shapes picked out in lead and different intensities and splashes of colour, even the absence of colour, successfully do the suggesting.

Although it is difficult to say for certain what the windows depict in terms of subject matter, the imagination with the use of Chagall's suggestions can come up with all sorts of things. There are figures, animals and plants. Perhaps Chagall is even playing with the viewer, allowing the creative mind to wander.

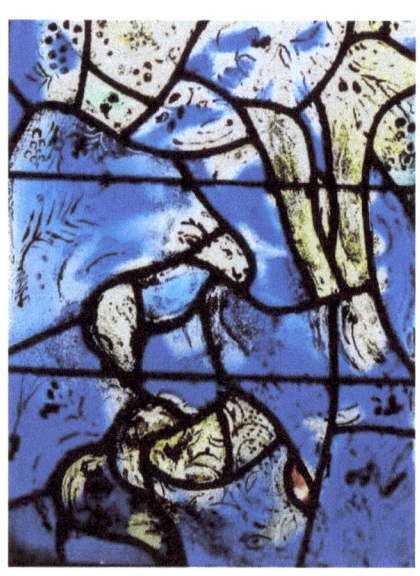

Abstract window detail

One of the strong images hints that it could be Adam and Eve at the tree of knowledge while another may be taken as Jonah in the stormy sea. One thing I find is that even though there is no real definition of the subjects undertaken, there is an awesome sense of spirituality in the space that they occupy. It is only because of the very obvious angelic figures and the environment being a church building that this space has a recognisable "religious" spirituality. If it weren't for preconceived ideas of religious imagery or buildings, these windows would, I believe, lead the viewer to a place of spirituality anyway.

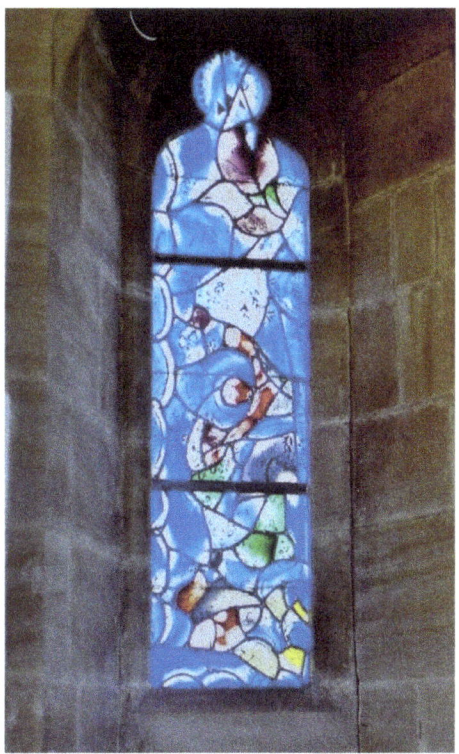

Abstract window possibly showing turbulent water

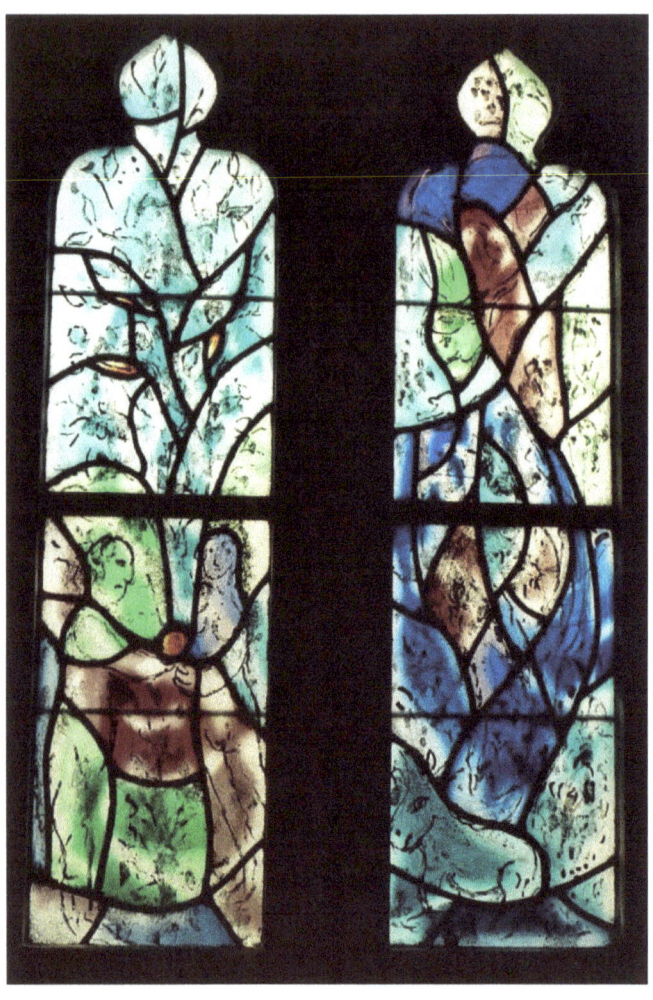

Abstract window possibly showing Adam and Eve with the tree of life

Before these windows were installed there existed other stained glass in their place. Chagall took into account that these had a religious message which would have been described as a "little more to the point than his work", however, when seen together these windows portray a more subtle approach with a strong spirituality. The abstractness of the windows does not distract, but instead they are more informative to the modern person who knows little about the biblical and religious scenes that are in older and more traditional stained glass.

At this point a little about the structure of the windows needs to be discussed.

Chagall said very little about the placement of the leads in his windows. Charles Marq, his wife and their assistants in Reims turned their skills to Chagall's maquettes. They took these scaled sketches and it was found that the leads should follow the maquette in three areas. These were colour, form and line. There are times when individual colours are enclosed and other times when a recognisable image is cut right through because of the blocks of coloured paper and strong directional movement of a brush stroke on the maquettes.

Chagall did not make the windows or the glass himself. This is attributed to Charles Marq and the team at Reims. The glass making was a slow and intricate process. Layers of colour were built up inside the glass. It could also be acid etched to remove areas of colour so that light could penetrate either in precise blocks or to delicately blend colours. Chagall did however, add the finishing touches once they were completed or installed. He endeavoured to bring them back to a closer reality of his initial maquettes by painting the tin based grisaille to the surface. He used a variety of brush strokes and finger painting in this medium that could be near translucent or deep black in colour.

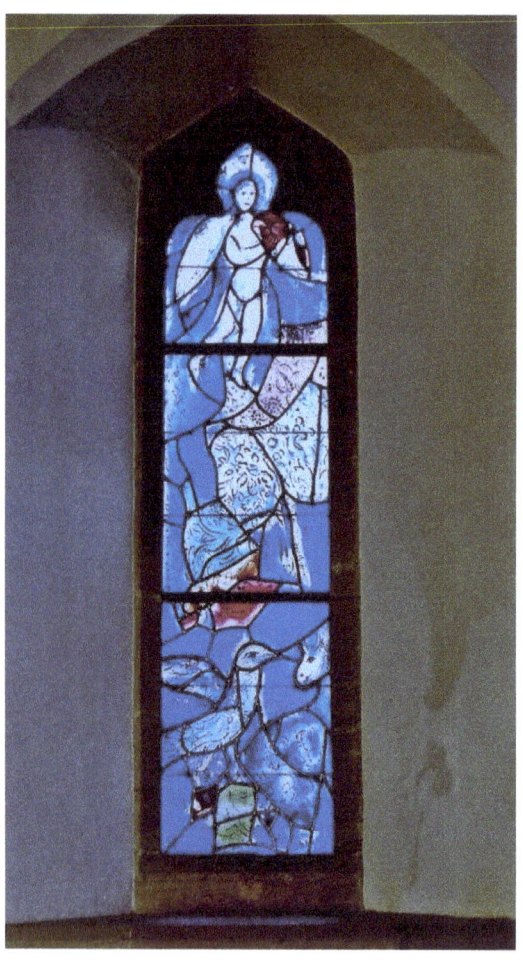

Abstract window in the chancel

Just past the pulpit you are focused once again. You are raised to a platform by a step, the ceiling above you drops a level and the vertical walls are pulled in. An edge is defined and another threshold must be crossed. The dropping of the ceiling emphasises and raises the platform even more. These actions concentrate the view of the chancel from the view of the previous nave.

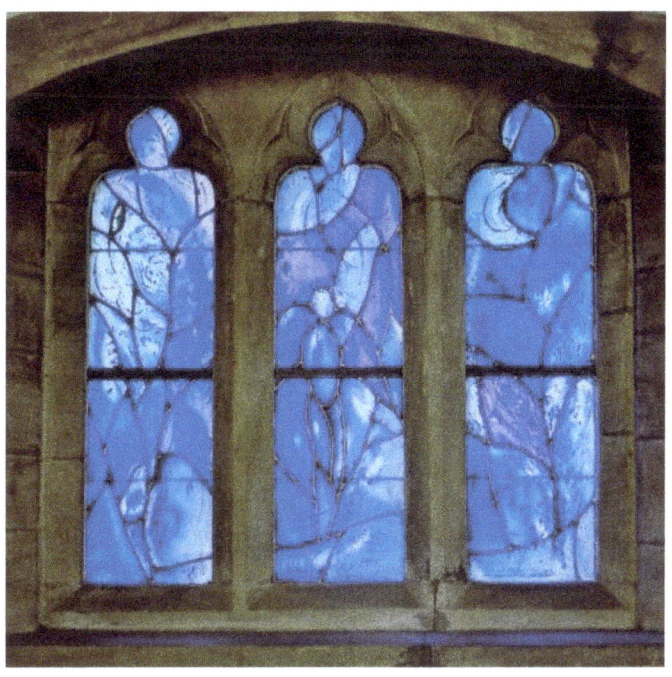

Abstract window under the arches

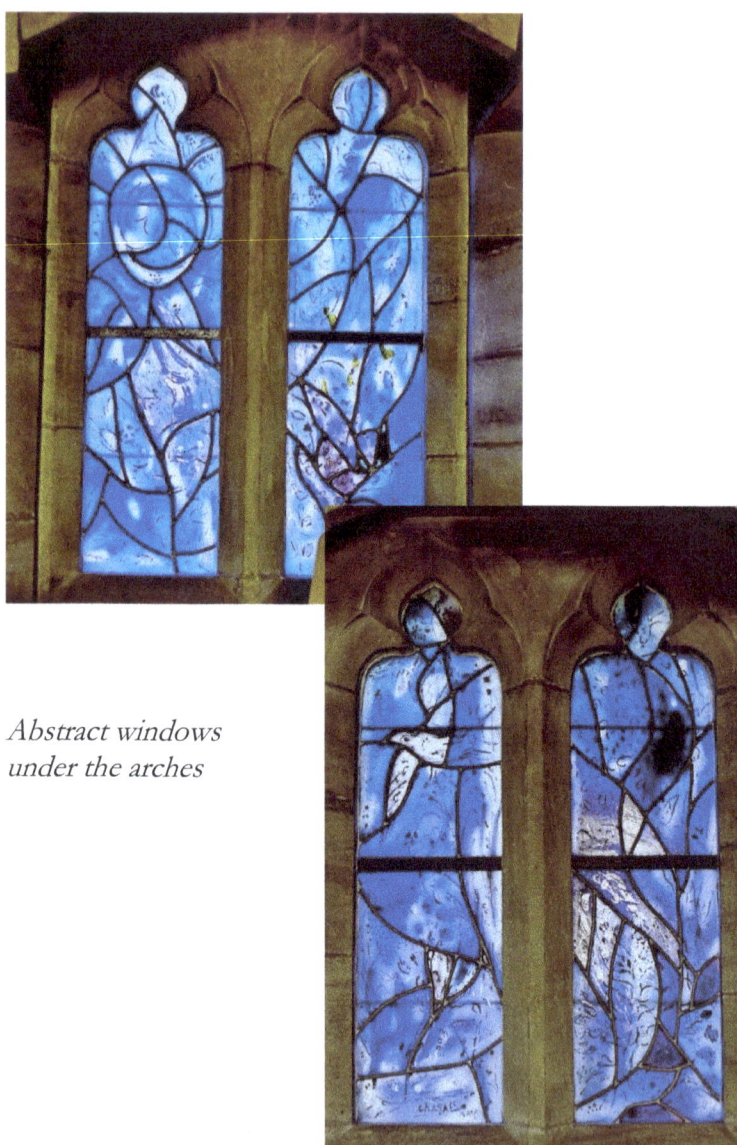

*Abstract windows
under the arches*

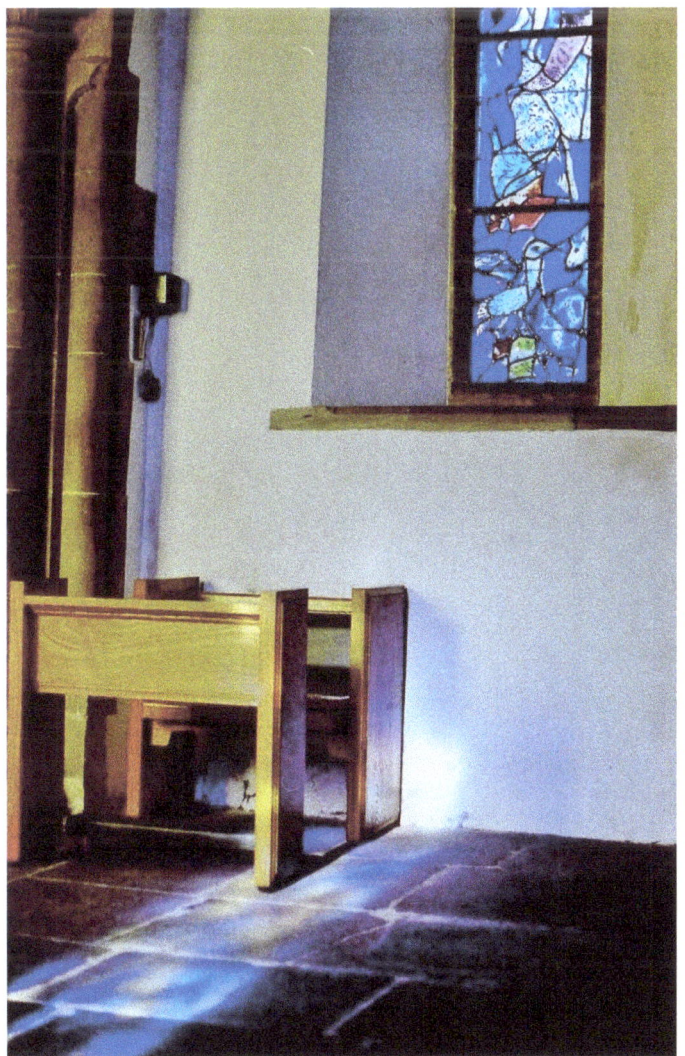

Light pours into the space

The chancel is free from furnishings except a tomb. The light through the windows here are predominately blue giving an emotion of peace and gentleness. The area seems hushed.

Two steps and a wooden railing separate you from the altar and the dedicated window in the east wall. There seems to be a barrier here, even though you can see what is being protected. This edge in not uneasy, it is penetrated by the coloured light from the window above. This space is prayerful.

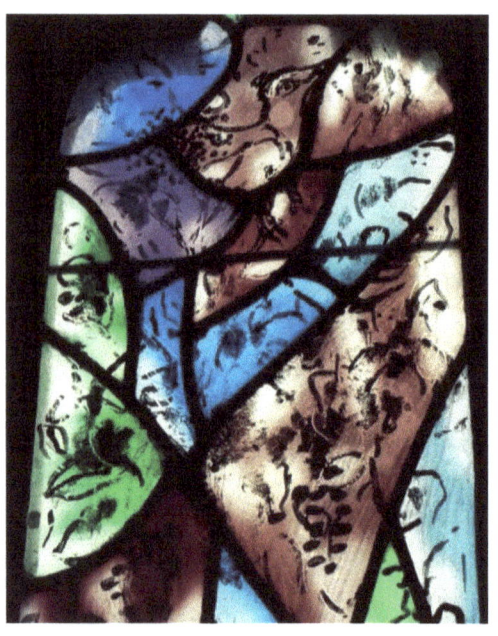

Detail from an abstract window

The East Window

In 1963, Sarah Venetia d'Avigdor Goldsmid and two friends died in a sailing accident. The east window of All Saints, her local church, was commissioned by her parents as a memorial to Sarah.

The window shows a young woman, Sarah, in the swirling waters, her mother looking on cradling her two other children. A friend in the right corner weeps.

Sarah is then borne to calmer waters where she begins to climb a ladder. At the top of the ladder are her two friends, already welcomed by Jesus Christ on the cross and a joyous angel. Jesus is depicted here as a young man, someone Sarah could relate to. Jesus, the angel and the ladder with someone climbing are familiar subjects. Chagall used the same imagery in the Good Samaritan window in Pocantico Hills.

There is also an image of Sarah riding a red horse which is said to represent calm and happiness[11]. Chagall says in Chagall by Chagall, *"At the sight of horses that are always in a state of ecstasy I wonder: are they perhaps happier than we?"*[12]. Sarah's horse in the window looks as though it is in a state of ecstasy and perhaps Chagall wants Sarah to know this happiness.

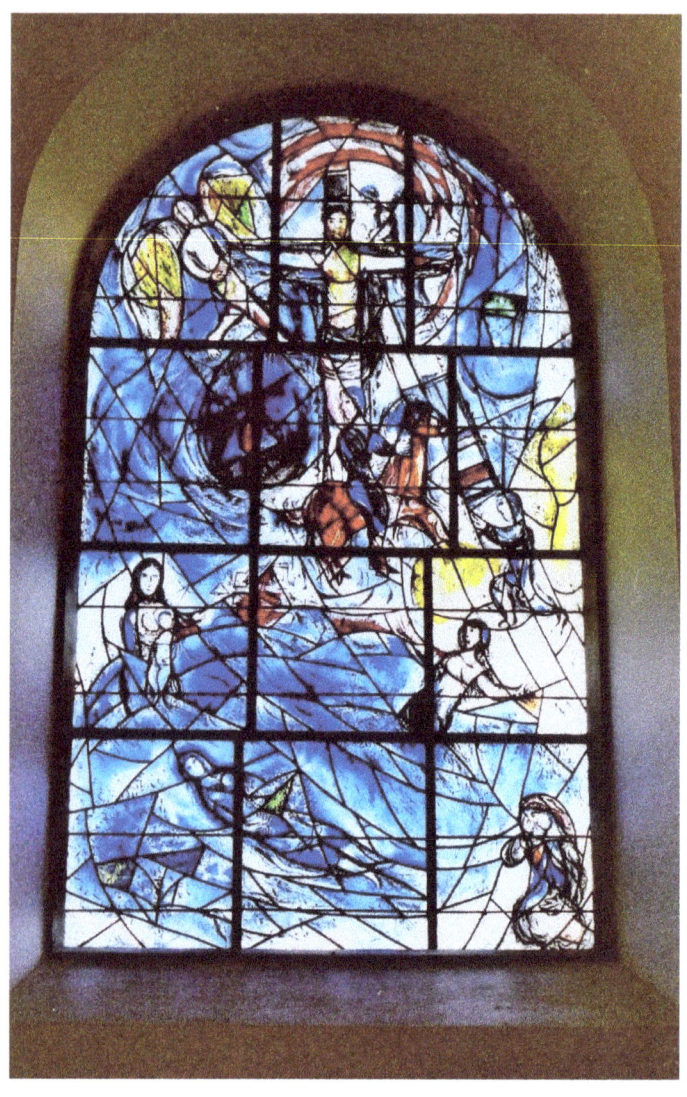

The East window – Memorial to Sarah

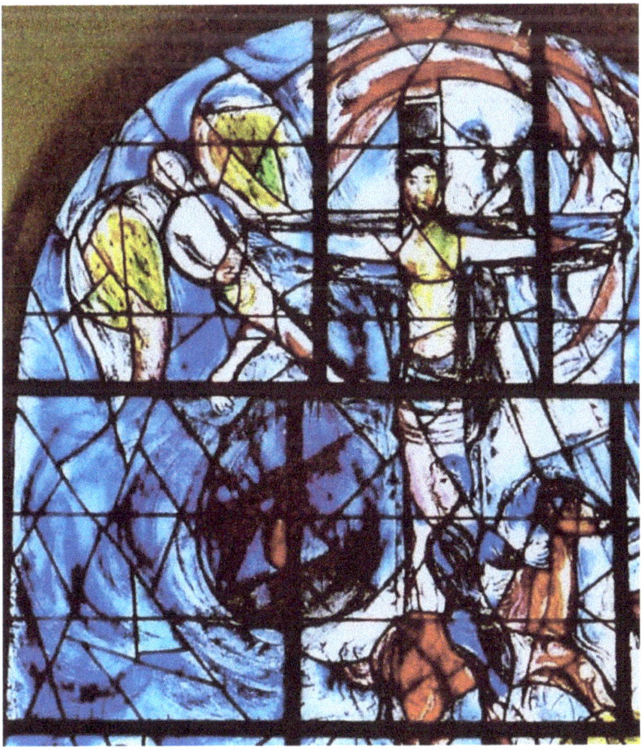

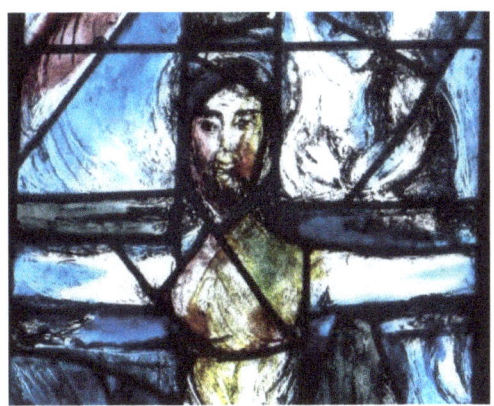

Details from the East Window

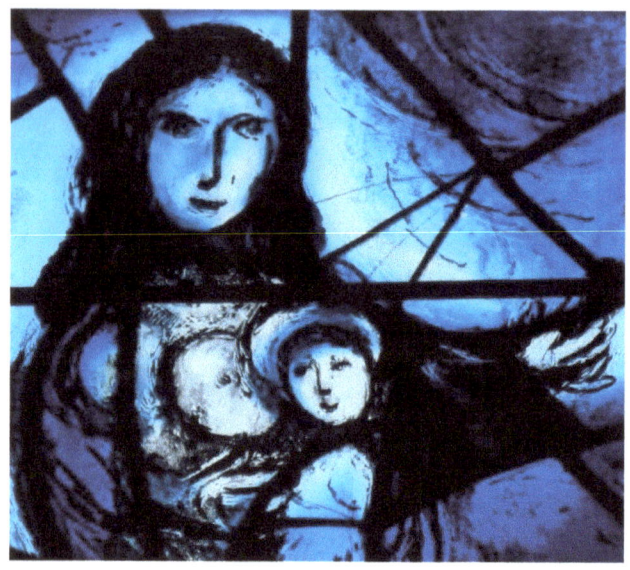

Details from the East Window

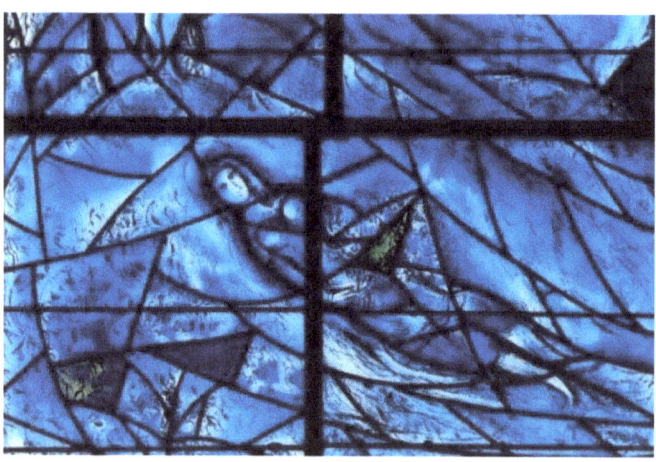

Chagall depicts Sarah looking backwards. She could be looking back to what she could have been, perhaps she does not want to leave or even be saying goodbye to her mother.

Chagall had seen death many times and he was saddened by it. He knew that he could not bring people back and each had a time to go even though he didn't understand why. This is why I feel that Sarah is saying goodbye, this was her time. The memorial window does not hold onto her but holds onto her memory.

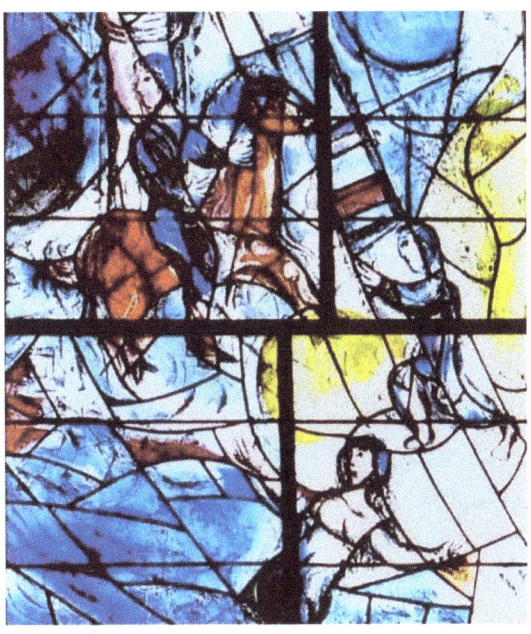

Detail of the red horse and ladder in the East Window

(Chagall's window in Chichester contained a king riding a horse and can be seen on page 13)

The horse in the window is similar to a horse painted in 1976 by Chagall in a painting "At the Circus". He said, "*I would surround her with my flowering and withering years … I would run after her horse to ask how to live, to escape from myself, from the world, to whom I run, where to go.*"[13] I think Chagall can relate to Sarah on her horse.

I do not proclaim the drama of life. I do not dramatise, even when death is present in a picture. It's tragic by nature, quite simply that's how it is. [14]

Chagall knew the tragedy of death. He had seen it. But in this window Chagall does not dwell on this tragedy. It is a window that celebrates a life, but also causes the viewer to question issues about their own life. Could it also be celebrated?

It is here that I feel is the centre of the church. The whole journey through the building, and the whole spiritual journey from praise to worship to prayer, leads here. Chagall used colour and suggestion to lead the viewer to this place and the place of questioning. Perhaps in this window he was trying to provide answers.

Marc Chagall was a Jew and I think he knew there was a need for this spiritual journey through the means of a physical journey.

Conclusion

Both church buildings have a few things in common. They each sit slightly off the beaten track, but are at the heart of certain communities, the regular church-goer and the self-confessed art critic. Chagall responded to the two very different environments in contrasting and similar ways.

In England the setting for his work was originally an old Saxon church building, which had since been adjusted and added to with very traditional stained glass installed. Chagall questioned the traditional approach and designed and installed a modern interpretation of traditional values incorporated in his work. This does not degrade the history of the place or make it a lesser place of worship, rather it enhances these qualities.

In America, with a western culture much like the English in some ways and yet also very different, Chagall reacted in a similar way. The church building in Pocantico Hills which is modern in comparison to Tudeley, received a traditionalised approach. Although when compared against the medieval examples of stained glass, the Prophets may appear at a tangent in design thinking, they are not. The subject matter that Chagall took on is very traditional. For the window to tell a story of a hero in the Bible is a very common subject found in windows all over the world. This time,

Chagall took the modern building and gave it some tradition.

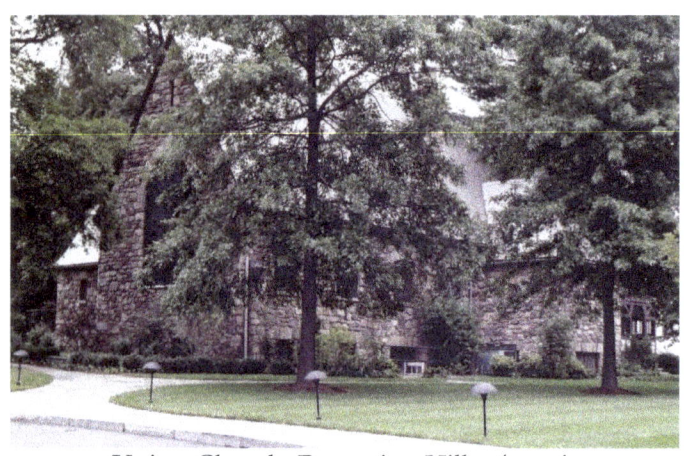

Union Church, Pocantico Hills, America

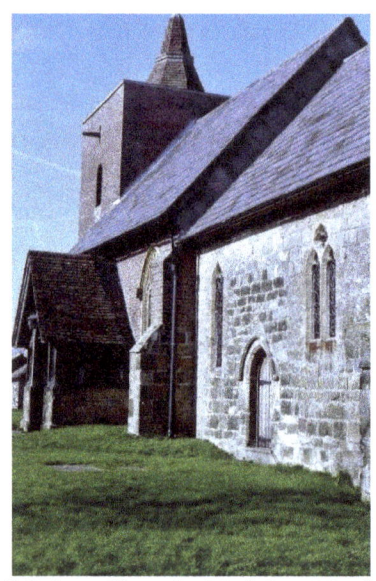

All Saints Church, Tudeley, England

To look at the windows within the context of the two buildings is very important. At Tudeley the journey through the building brings the viewer eventually to a place of prayer and meditation through the means of experience of the window's form and colour. In Pocantico Hills, this same journey is attempted, although a little more awkwardly through the poses and attitude of the prophets.

Chagall said:

"… to the best of my ability, in the course of my life – though I sometimes have the impression that I am someone else entirely, that I was born one might say between heaven and earth, that the world for me is a great torch – I have painted these pictures in keeping with that remote dream. I wanted to leave then in this House so that men may try to find here a certain peace, a certain spirituality, a religious feeling, a sense of life.

To my mind, these paintings do not represent the dream of a single people but of all mankind.

It is not for me to comment on them. Works of art must speak for themselves.

We often speak of style, in what forms, what movements to place colour. But this colour is something innate. It depends neither on style nor on the form in which you put it.

Neither does it depend on your skill with the brush." [15]

Chagall understood that he was not just a physical being but that there was something inside him that cried out to something else. He felt that all mankind had the same cry.

He also understood that it is important to give an introduction to God. With all the daily pressures that people face there is a need to shake off those distractions and focus on God. Chagall did this through a means of the viewer's personal insight or interpretation of his work.

The windows in America were designed before the windows in England. The time difference between these two projects, and the lack of intermediate projects, meant that Chagall had time to dwell more deeply in this subject matter and style. Both of these commissions were for churches and enabled Chagall to bring progression to his work. Chagall moved on from the work at Pocantico Hills and progressed further in his windows at Tudeley. He attempted to bring a spiritual journey into the experience of the American church through individual commissions. This was a difficult brief to fulfil. The individual windows needed to have strong individual meaning for each memorial to be special. The spiritual journey was therefore achieved through the strength of images. In England the brief was more simple and freeing and he could achieve this journey through whatever means he preferred.

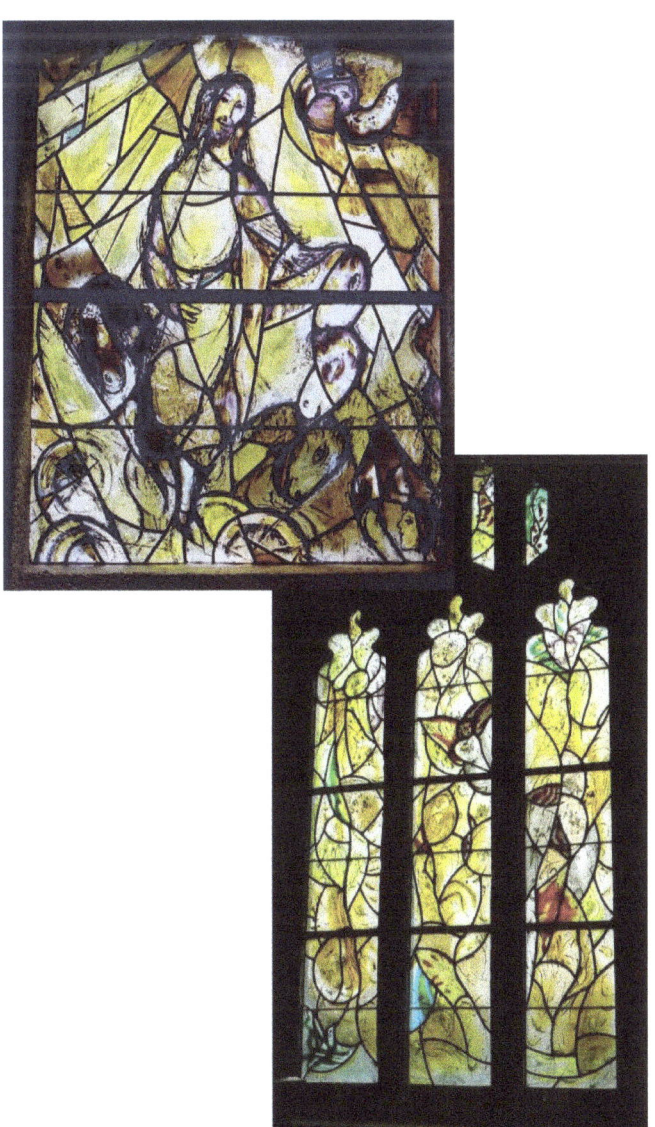

Top: The Prophet Elijah – Pocantico Hills
Below: Abstract window near entrance – Tudeley

The differences of the brief mean that the Pocantico Hills experience is very different to that of Tudeley.

In Pocantico Hills the spiritual journey is very much hidden by the upfront stories of the Prophets. It is easy, therefore, to break down the building in to sections even though it is seen as one large space. Below this, however, the journey does exist within the stories, attitudes and colours.

At Tudeley the journey is very much an emotional experience, using different spaces and colour. The thresholds within the building created by design are over-ridden by the emotional thresholds within the spiritual journey.

The short time elapsing from each commission allows us to see the similarities emerging. With Tudeley there are many snippets from the windows in Pocantico Hills. There are examples of doves and angels, although these do appear in many other examples of Chagall's work. One obvious copy or adaptation is found in the two main windows, The Good Samaritan and the East Window. Chagall uses the images of the crucifixion, ladder, angels and people in both.

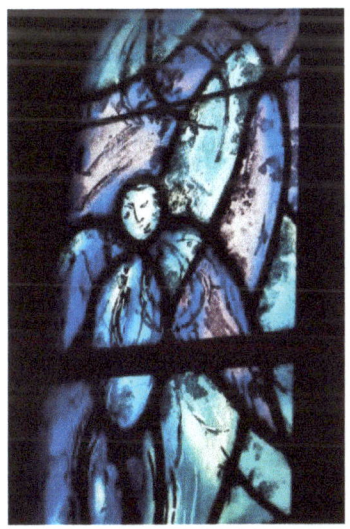
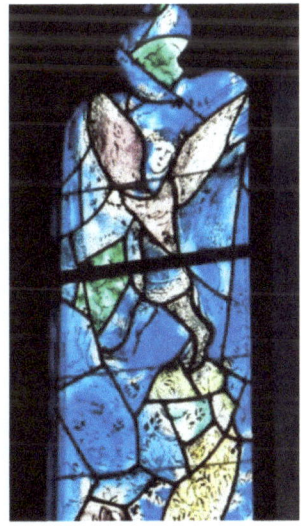
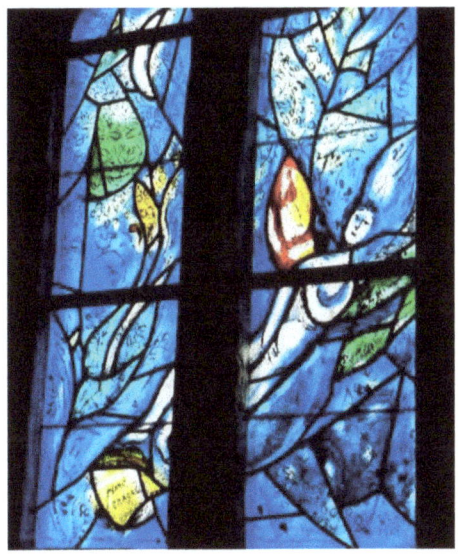

Examples of Angels in the abstract windows at Tudeley

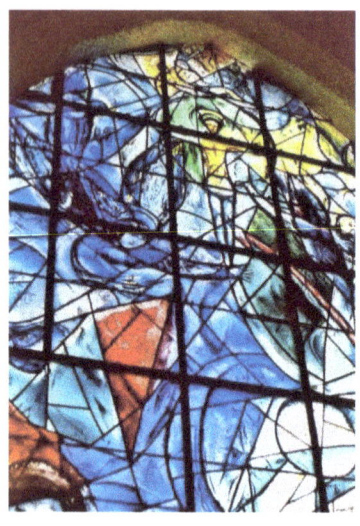

Jesus on the cross at Pocantico Hills

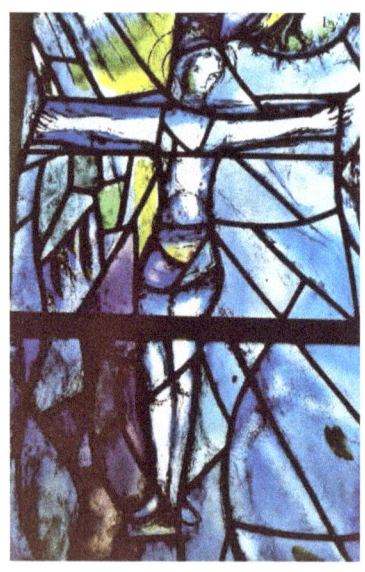

When Chagall speaks of the crucifixion, it is in the same breath that he mentions love or associates it with something he loves. He understands that the act of sacrificing yourself for others is a pure act of love.

And even today, when I paint a crucifixion or other religious picture, I experience again almost the same sensations that I felt while painting circus people, and yet there is nothing literary in these paintings, and it is very difficult to explain why I find a psycho-plastic resemblance between the two kinds of composition.[16]

How often I've thought of making my colours flow so that they become a river, of throwing across this river a bridge over which I would have liked to walk ad like Him to speak of love and crucifixion.[17]

Like Christ, I am crucified, fastened to my easel with nails.[18]

In his windows the crucifixion is that of Jesus (in some of his paintings he has also shown other subjects crucified). This was a love sacrifice. It is the centre of the Christian belief, but it is not just because of this that Chagall chose to use the imagery. He found for himself the importance of scripture.

I see the events of life and works of art through the wisdom of the Bible. A truly great work is penetrated by its spirit and harmony. I am probably not the only one to think so, especially in our times.[19]

Since in my inner life the spirit and the world of the Bible occupy a large place, I have tried to express it. It is essential to show the elements of the world that are not visible and not to reproduce nature in all its aspects.

Chagall was a Jew, yet he had an interest in the New Testament as well as the old which is uncommon since the Jewish faith bases its belief on the Old Testament. He tried to express the act of love at the crucifixion of Jesus.

His other images of the person climbing the ladder surrounded by angels, not only express the hope of the Christian faith but also the hope of his own heart. The ascending suggests moving up to something else. The Christian belief is that of eternal life after death. The subject at Tudeley was that of Sarah's death, therefore the ladder symbolises the hope of eternal life after death. The fact that he returned to this subject at Tudeley, and making it much more prominent in the window suggests that he had the need to re-emphasise, re-write, bring together, underscore and even understand this message. This may help the church gathered there to understand, but he also did it for himself.

Over the years the two sites have come into the tourism business. Each has dealt with it in different ways. Chagall's work brings people to the church building which may appear to be a great idea. However, the symbol of this type of building to the everyday person is a place of gentleness and quietness, after all it is not a modern style church or a refined and spacious art gallery. Can these buildings put up with the feet of Chagall's pilgrims? Should these works of art be in another place, like a gallery? To that, the answer must be, "No!" To remove these windows from this context would be to remove part of their meaning. They need to be seen as a whole in these places of worship for which they were conceived and designed so eloquently. These buildings will have to continue to protect the windows, now achieved by the fitting of armour- plated glass (there have been attacks on the American windows). The churches will be perceived by some as an art gallery and just visited but to others these buildings are a place of worship and need to be respected. There must be a careful balance; the art gallery attitude must not overtake the use of the building to the local parishioners. Chagall's windows inhabit a place of worship to God and not art.

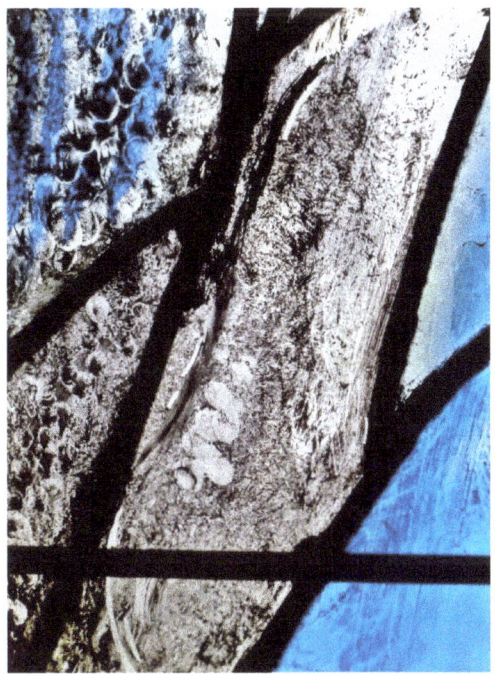

Detail from Ezekiel at Pocantico Hill, showing the fingerprints of Marc Chagall

End-Notes

[1] Chagall by Jean Cassou, page 26, paragraph 1
Publisher – Thames and Hudson London 1965
Translated from the French by Alisa Jaffa

[2] The History of All Saints Church, Tudeley in the County of Kent, Section The Restoration of 1966-1967 and the Stained Glass Windows of Marc Chagall, page 3, paragraph 4
Publisher – Addax Publishing Limited 1994

[3] Historical background interpreted by the author from A Brief History of the Union Church of Pocantico Hills

[4] The Message by Eugene Peterson
Publisher – Navpress 1993

The following are taken from Chagall by Chagall
Publisher – New English Library Limited 1979
Edited by Charles Sortier
Translated from the French by John Shepley
[5] Page 199
[12] Page 174, paragraph 6
[13] Page 176, paragraph 2 & 3
[14] Page 199
[15] Page 189, paragraph 1, 2 & 3
[16] Page 185, paragraph 2
[17] Page 219, paragraph 2
[19] Page 193, paragraph 2

[6] Bible quotes taken from the New International Version unless otherwise stated

[7] The Twelve Chagall Windows, page 8, paragraph 6
[8] The Twelve Chagall Windows, page 11, paragraph 4
Publisher – Haddassah Medical Organisation in Israel

[9] Nine Windows by Chagall, narrative to the exhibition at the Museum of Modern Art, New York, 1978, paragraph 3.

[10] Painting in Light by Susan Moore, page 591, paragraph 2
Publisher – Counrty Life, 06 March 1986, volume 179, number 4620, pages 590-591

[11] The History of All Saints Church, Tudeley in the County of Kent, Section The Restoration of 1966-1967 and the Stained Glass Windows of Marc Chagall, page 3, paragraph 4
Publisher – Addax Publishing Limited 1994

[18] Marc Chagall by Franz Meyer, page 383
Publisher – New York: Harry N Adams

Bibliography – Books

Arnold, Hugh
Stained Glass of the Middle Ages in
England and France
London
Adam and Charles Black
1939

Cassou, Jean
Chagall
London
Thames and Hudson
1965
Translated from the French by
Alisa Jaffa

Chagall, Marc
Chagall by Chagall
New English Library Limited
1979
Edited by Charles Sortier
Translated from the French by
John Shepley

Clarke, Brian – Editor
Architectural Stained Glass
London
Murray
1979

Lee, Lawerence
The Appreciation of Stained Glass
London
Oxford University Press
1977

Moor, Andrew
Contemporary Stained Glass: a
guide to the potential of modern
stained glass in architecture

Newman, John
West Kent and the Weald
Harmondsworth
Penguin
1969
Edited by Nikolaus Pevsner

Sewter, Albert Charles
The Stained Glass of William
Morris and his Circle
London
Yale University Press for Paul
Mellon Centre for Studies in British
Art (London) Ltd
1974

Sewers, Robert
Stained Glass: An Architectural Art
New York, U.S.A.
Universe Books
1965

Lee, Lawrence, Sedden, George,
Stephens, Francis
Stained Glass
London
Mitchell Beazley
1976

Bibliography – Articles

Alsop, S.M.
"Architecture: Wilthrop Faulkner"
Architectural Digest
Volume 50, pages 146-149
July 1993

Alsop, S.M.
"Legend of Kykuit: The Rockfellers' Pocantico Hills Estate Prepares to Open its Gates"
Architectural Digest
Volume 49 pages 136-147
May 1992

Dean, Andrea Oppenheimer
"Obituary"
Architecture
Volume 74, pages 108-111
May 1985

Freeman, A
"The Coming of Kykuit"
Historic Preservation
Volume 44, pages 26-35, 77
July August 1992

Friedman, Mira
"Marc Chagall's Portrayal of the Prophet Jerimiah"
Zeitschrift Fur Kunstgeschichte
Volume 47, number 3, pages 374-391
1984

Freidman, Mira
"The Tree of Jesse and the Tree of Life in Chagall"
Jewish Art
Volume 15, pages 61-80
1989

McNally, Janet
"Chagall in Glass"
Stained Glass (American)
Volume 80, number 3, pages 227-231

Moore, Susan
"Painting in Light"
Country Life
Volume 179, number 4620, pages 590-591
06 March 1986

Nel, T
"Church Lighting"
South African Architectural Record
Pages 15-17
January 1967

Salmon, Karen
"National Building: Museum Honours Rockefeller Family"
Architecture
Volume 80, pages 36-37
May 1991

Waldram
"The Lighting of Churches"
International Lighting Review (Amsterdam)
Number 5, pages 200-205
1965

www.ingramcontent.com/pod-product-compliance
Lightning Source LLC
Chambersburg PA
CBHW040952170526
45159CB00013B/3112